Missionary Principles

Other books by Roland Allen

MISSIONARY METHODS: ST. PAUL'S OR OURS?

THE SPONTANEOUS EXPANSION OF THE CHURCH
AND THE CAUSES WHICH HINDER IT

Missionary Principles

by

ROLAND ALLEN

WILLIAM B. EERDMANS PUBLISHING COMPANY
GRAND RAPIDS, MICHIGAN

PREFACE

IF I have attempted to restate a few commonplace truths, let their frequent neglect be my excuse: if in restating I have untruthed any, let my censure be their restoration.

R. A.

CONTENTS

CHAPTER I

CHAPTER II

THE HOPE

CHAPTER III

CHAPTER IV

THE IMPULSE

MISSIONARY PRINCIPLES

CHAPTER I

The Impulse

WE are sometimes surprised that men who call themselves the servants of Christ appear to be wholly unmoved by the command of Christ to preach the Gospel to all nations. The command is clear; it is repeated again and again.[1] Christians do not question its authority; they do not doubt that Christ gave it; they do not doubt His right to give it; they simply disobey it. The command does not come home to them. It does not appear to have any binding force. This seems strange. We think that the

[1] St. Matt. xxviii. 19-20; St. Mark xvi. 15; St. Luke xxiv. 47; St. John xx. 21; Acts i. 8.

mere repetition of the command should be enough.

I. When we so think or speak we are treating the command of Christ as if it were a law of the same order as the laws of Judaism or of any other legal system. But there is a difference between the commands of Christ, the laws of the Gospel, and the commands of the Law. It is a difference not of form but of essence. The commands of the Law are external, the commands of the Gospel are internal. The commands of the Law are given from without, the commands of the Gospel are implanted. It is the promise of the Old Testament, " I will write my laws in their hearts " ; the fulfilment of the promise is found only in the New Testament.

The fact that there are in the Old Testament some commands which seem to anticipate the Gospel, and that in the New Testament there are some commands which seem to belong in character to the Old Testament does not invalidate this distinction

any more than the fact that some members
of the vegetable kingdom possess characteristics proper to the animal kingdom and
that some members of the animal kingdom
possess characteristics proper to members
of the vegetable kingdom invalidates the
distinction between the animal and vegetable
kingdoms.

(a) Divine laws are the expression in
words of the will of God for man. Under
a legal system it is the external form, the
word, which is communicated to men. So
expressed the Spirit is limited by the weakness of human speech. A Spirit once set
down as Law is necessarily imperfect. The
word fixes an arbitrary standard, a definite
point, a maximum or a minimum, above or
below which action is forbidden Under
Law the command is bound up with the
Letter, the written word. The Letter is the
standard. But in Gospel this is not so.
Under Gospel it is the Spirit which is communicated. In Gospel the Spirit is the
standard. Gospel law is not a form of words :

B

it is an ideal with no fixed point. In Gospel any expression in words is subject to the Spirit. Consequently the very verbal expression changes its content to the eye of the soul as the soul more and more realizes the impulse of the Spirit.

This does not alter the fact that in Gospel there are points below which a man cannot fall without revealing that he has not the Spirit. The Spirit in the Body recognizes such points. There is a point at which failure proclaims that a man has denied the faith and is worse than an infidel. But even this is not a fixed point. It varies from age to age and from place to place.

If the command to go into all the world were a command of the Law it would be bound by the letter of the words " go " and " the world." Certainly it could be obeyed only by physical and material " going." But the " going " demanded by the Spirit is essentially a spiritual process which is far wider and fuller than any material going. Men do not necessarily "go into all the world " when they go as missionaries to China or to Africa, or to any other place. It is possible to be as " narrow " in Africa as in one's native village. It is possible to circumnavigate the globe without " going into the world " at all. Spiritual going is not less real than physical but more real. Christ came into " the world " though He walked in the flesh in Palestine alone. We ought to " go " as Christ " came." It is because we do not think of this, because we treat the command as the law of a legal system, which sets up a standard bound by the letter, that we do not understand it. We see that as it stands literally it is impossible. How often do we hear it quoted with the commentary, " Of course we cannot all go." We do not therefore leap for joy in the presence of a spiritual truth revealed to us. We speak as if a man who goes physically to some foreign country fulfils the command more *really* than the man who stays at home. We whittle it away. We interpret " go " as " send " or " give." We sometimes speak of " a substitute," as if one

soul could do another soul's duty, as one man
under a legal system here on earth might
serve as substitute for another in military
service.   Of course I do not deny that acts of
" going " or " giving " or " sending " may
all be expressions in outward form of a real
spiritual " going."   Of course they may be.
But the command is not " obeyed " by
these outward acts.   " Go ye into all the
world " is not a legal phrase local and temporal which can be so obeyed.   The Spirit
is not bound by material local and temporal
chains, any more than by the letter of a law.
We miss much, I fancy, by this material form
of speech.   I wonder what would happen
if we all went " into all the world " in the
places where we were born or to which the
Spirit might carry us, receiving a world-wide
Spirit and expressing a world-wide Spirit
wherever we might be.   That many of us
would move about the world is as certain as
that Christ moved from Galilee to Judaea ;
but wherever we were we should go into all
the world.

(*b*) Obedience to the commands of the Gospel is a spiritual act. The Gospel law is a law of liberty, that is, a law of internal life not of external compulsion. It is the law which rules the active expression of a spirit making its own proper free response to the will of God. This was the obedience of Christ. Christ says : " As the Father hath sent Me, even so send I you." [1] How then did the Father send the Son ? By a command ? Certainly by a command. Christ speaks of a command, " As the Father gave Me commandment even so I do." [2] But not by an external command. Christ speaks more often of a community of will, " My meat is to do the will of Him that sent Me." The Father sent the Son by a command ; but the command was a Procession of the Holy Ghost. The Spirit of the Father who sent was the Spirit of the Son who came. The command was an expression of the Spirit and the response was the expression of the same Spirit ; because there was community

[1] St. John xx. 21.   [2] St. John xiv. 31.

of Spirit ; for the Spirit proceeds from the
Father and from the Son.   So Christ sends
His people into the world not by an external
command only ; but by a giving of the same
Spirit, " He breathed on them." [1]

Obedience is the acceptance of this gift,
the surrender of ourselves to this Spirit.
Legal commands do not demand this internal
surrender, this acceptance of a gift, as the
condition of their fulfilment.   All that they
require is external obedience.   If the outward
act is not in contradiction to the letter of the
law, the internal condition is not regarded.
Willing obedience and unwilling are alike
obedience.   A legal system is a slave driver.
If what the slave driver demands of the
slave is done, he cares not for the motive
from which it is done.   But unwilling
obedience to Gospel commands is not obedience at all.   It is indeed a contradiction in
terms.   Obedience to the command to preach
the Gospel to all nations except as an expression of the Spirit of Christ indwelling

[1] St John xx. 22.

the soul is an absurdity, a contradiction of itself.

(c) Legal commands do not demand this internal surrender, this acceptance of a gift, as the condition of their fulfilment, because they have no such gift to offer. An external command cannot be an impulse, a motive for action. A command may suggest a motive, but it is not, and cannot be, a motive in itself. A command is a stick, or a whip, which appeals to some feeling which can respond to it, just as the nervous system responds to a blow. A command presupposes a spirit which can respond to its appeal; but whilst it presupposes a spirit to which it can appeal, it does not presuppose the spirit of the command. The law is not made for the righteous man, but for the unrighteous. Therefore the law appeals to some motive which can produce the right action; but which is not itself the spirit of the right action. The law is made because the spirit of the right action is absent, and therefore the right action would not be taken without some other appeal. Hence the Law rests upon sanctions. It endeavours to lead men into the right path by threatening them with punishments if they transgress, or by promising them rewards if they obey. In this way Law substitutes some other motive for the spirit of the command.

The Gospel on the other hand supplies the motive. In the Gospel the Spirit which expresses Himself in the command is given to the soul to whom the command is addressed. The command is an expression of the mind of the Spirit. It is an instruction in the character of the Spirit given. Thus in the Gospel the command does not appeal to another motive which is not the spirit of the command. In the New Testament the gospel is the offer of a free gift of grace. Those who refuse it remain under law and its threats ; those who accept it are no longer under law, they are under grace. The threats of the Gospel are addressed not to those who receive the grace but to those who reject it and refuse to follow it. They

are rather warnings of the consequences of
refusing the grace. Thus under Gospel
there are no sanctions. To those under
grace it threatens no punishment other than
the terror of falling from grace : it offers no
reward to those who accept it other than its
own fulfilment, which is their supreme bliss.

So the command to preach the Gospel
has no sanction. It is clearly associated
with the promise of the presence of Christ
with His people, " Lo I am with you alway "; [1]
with the gift of power from on high, " Ye
shall receive power " ; [2] with the coming of the
Holy Ghost, " He shall bear witness, and ye
also shall bear witness " ; [3] but the promise
of the presence of Christ, the gift of the indwelling Spirit, is not a reward offered to
those who obey : it is the assurance that
those who are commanded will be able to
obey. It is the promise of the motive power
to which the command appeals. The voice
of Christ without the soul speaks to the

[1] St. Matt. xxviii. 20.   [2] Acts i. 8.
[3] St. John xv. 26–27.

Spirit of Christ within the soul. Christ first gives the Spirit and then the command. He first comes to us, and then commands us to go.

This manner of command is peculiar to the Gospel. The essential characteristic of the Gospel is that it is an administration of the Spirit. On the reality of this coming of the Holy Ghost turns not only the whole meaning and purpose and manner and power of Foreign Missions ; but the very existence and character of our religion. We do not propagate a new system of theology and ethics, because the Gospel which was preached to us was not a new system of theology and ethics. It was because St. Paul would never for one instant allow that the Gospel which he preached was such a system that his whole life was one long martyrdom.

(a) It is by this that Christianity is separated from all other religions. It stands apart, in a class by itself, distinct from all others, not merely in the fulness of its truth and the height of its moral teaching, but in its essential character. Christ did not merely impart a doctrine more true, more exalted than Moses, or Confucius, or the Buddha or any others who had preceded Him. He did not merely introduce a new understanding of the Nature of God and of the manner of approach to Him. He imparted His own Spirit, He implanted His own Divine Life in the souls of His people. The others gave commands ; they taught with more or less truth what men ought to be and do, and their systems may be compared one with another because they are in the same order. But it is impossible to compare a system of directions with a Spirit. It is impossible to put into the same class commands and motives. They gave commands : Christ gives motive power. They told men what they ought to do : Christ imparts the Spirit from which the command emanates. Their commands remained an external burden to be taken up with sorrow and laid down with despair : Christ gives an internal power which grows stronger and stronger and works out our

salvation in Him.   They gave words : Christ
gives Himself.   The one thing that is vital
for the Christian is not wisdom, nor ritual
observance, but union with Christ.   The one
thing for which Christians pray, the one
thing which in the last resort is needful, is
that Christ shall dwell in our hearts.   In that
Presence lies the secret of life, of power, of
service, of response to the commands of
Christ.

Nearly all the objections commonly raised
against Foreign Missions have their root in a
fundamental objection to this supreme claim
of Christ, to this essential character of
Christianity.   The Jews rejected Christ and
His righteousness because they preferred
their own righteousness, the righteousness
which men think to claim as their own as the
results of their own efforts to keep Law.   We
to-day accept Christ in name, but we often
reject His grace and refuse His righteousness in our thought and speech and deed.
When men talk of the Christian missionary
as a man who goes about to persuade others

that the religion in which they were brought up is a bad one and that the religion which he teaches is a better; when they say that Eastern nations have religions which are good for them, whilst we in the West have a religion which is good for us; when they question the value of educating the natives of any country in our religion on the ground that they cannot understand, appreciate, or follow it properly; they are treating Christianity as a system of ethics and theology, better perhaps than the systems of the non-Christian world, at least for us, but essentially of the same order. In other words they are not speaking of the Gospel at all, but of a philosophical and legal system. The Christianity of the Apostles was not such. For them the one thing of vital necessity for the salvation of souls was that they should receive the Spirit. All righteousness, all hope of righteousness, had its source and spring in the indwelling Spirit of Christ the righteous.

(b) This is the essential character of the

Gospel and therefore I suppose it is that, in this matter of spreading the Gospel, St. Paul never appeals to the command of Christ. This has seemed strange to many. But it is only an illustration of the attitude of the Apostle to all Law as Law.[1] His conception of the Gospel as a dispensation of Spirit forbade him to rely upon the letter of any command. Even in cases where there was danger of gross immorality he did not appeal to law as providing a motive for right conduct. He appealed to the Spirit, " Know ye not that your body is a Temple of the Holy Ghost ? "[2]

Because the missionary command is a command of the Gospel not of the Law, it would appear to be a mistake to speak of the missionary work of the Church as a duty based upon a command, or of the evangelization of the world as an obligation laid upon the Church by her Lord, as though this duty or obligation in any sense depended upon any particular word of the Lord.

[1] See *Missionary Methods*, ch. x.
[2] 1 Cor. vi. 19.

(*a*) In that case, if it were ever possible that it could be shown that the Lord gave no such command, or if Christians began seriously to doubt whether He ever used this or that particular form of words, then the obligation and the duty would perish with the letter of the command. But that is absurd. It would be far more true to say that had the Lord not given any such command, had the Scriptures never contained such a form of words, or could Christians blot it out from their Bibles and from their memories, the obligation to preach the Gospel to all nations would not have been diminished by a single iota. For the obligation depends not upon the letter, but upon the Spirit of Christ ; not upon what He orders, but upon what He is, and the Spirit of Christ is the Spirit of Divine love and compassion and desire for souls astray from God. The command appeals to that Spirit. But to turn from the Spirit and to appeal to the command, is to transpose the whole order and meaning of the Gospel. It is to appeal to the dead for life, to expect from an external command the virtue of an internal motive. It is to misuse the word of the Lord.

(b) To rely upon the letter of the command is to make that appear to be arbitrary which is really essential. A command which has no authority except the word of him who utters it is an arbitrary command. It need not have been uttered. It is conceivable that change of circumstances might lead to its withdrawal. It does not belong to the essential order of things. So it used to be argued that the obligation to preach the gospel to all nations ceased with the miraculous gifts of the Apostles. But Christ's command is not arbitrary. It could not have been unuttered. It is the voice of the Spirit of Christ in Him and in us. If the Spirit had not spoken through His mouth, He would still be speaking in our souls. If Christ had not said " Go into all the world," the word " Go into all the world " is so manifestly the expression of the Spirit of the Incarnation that whoever had first uttered it would have been instantly recognized as the mouthpiece of the Spirit. The whole Church would have accepted it as the voice of the Lord. The Spirit is prior to the letter. The letter does not create the Spirit but the Spirit the letter. And it could not change with changing circumstances, because though the circumstances may change the Spirit does not change. Jesus Christ is the same yesterday, to-day and for ever. And the Spirit of Jesus Christ is the Spirit of sacrifice. The Spirit which proceeds, goes, eternally goes forth in sacrifice, a Spirit of Love which eternally desires and strives for the welfare of all.

Nevertheless we are constantly tempted to base our appeal for help in missionary work upon the letter of the command. This is easy, because in form Gospel commands necessarily have an appearance of legality. " Go into all the world," " Do this in remembrance of Me," seems as legal as, " Thou shalt drive out the Hittite," or, " Thou shalt keep the Passover." Both as expressed in words are necessarily bounded by the weakness of human speech. The gift of the Spirit cannot be expressed in legal form, and we naturally tend to look on the outward things. Consequently we take the word for the Spirit.

When we do this we destroy the very foundations upon which alone any successful issue can be built. We destroy the Gospel command and make it legal. It actually becomes that which we make it. The moment that we treat a command of the Gospel expressed in words as a form of words, we make it an ordinance of the Law. The legal mind transmutes the object of thought. The command ceases to be Gospel and becomes Law.

But as legal the command is weak; as St. Paul says all law is weak through the flesh. It cannot be a motive; it cannot give life; it is a burden. It has not even the support of a sanction. As Gospel, the commands " Do this," " Go ye," are God's windows through which the Spirit shines;

as legal they need the added terror, "If
any man obey not, that soul shall be cut off.
He hath broken my covenant"; and there
is no such added terror. What wonder if
they are disregarded! As legal they have
no spiritual force. It is the service of the
Law to convict men as transgressors, not
to save them.

(c) So men break, so men always have
broken the law to the grief and disappoint-
ment of the priests of the law. We fail to
see that the failure is the natural result of the
system. We are often surprised to find that,
in doing what we most deplore, men are acting
strictly in accordance with the principles
which we have inculcated. We did not
anticipate that their action might be as
natural a consequence of the mode of our
presentation of the truth as the action
which we imagined must inevitably follow.
Here, for instance, if we treat the command
"Go ye" as an external direction, if we
bow to it ourselves as an external direction,
we expect all others to do the same. But

to our dismay when they hear it they do not bow to it. They do not even pay it the attention necessary to evoke a positive refusal to obey. They treat it as an external direction, just as we did. They put it on one side because it is an external direction which does not appeal to them, and is destitute of any powerful sanction. To us the command is a whip, or a goad. To them it is a whip without a lash, a pointless goad.

We invite this response when we treat that as legal which is really spiritual.

II. The command is not obeyed as a legal command, because it is not a legal command; it is not obeyed as a spiritual command, because the Nature of the Spirit is not explicitly realized and taught.

The Spirit which Christ imparts is the Spirit of which this command is the proper expression. He is the Spirit of the command. The command is a missionary command, the Spirit is a missionary Spirit. The first lesson which we learn in our earliest childhood about the Lord is that He, the Divine Son,

dwelling in the Light which no man can
approach unto in the bosom of the Father,
was impelled by that Spirit to abandon the
glory of Heaven and to come down into the
world in order to bring back in Himself
souls that had gone astray from the Father.
All His life and all His work, as it is seen
in the Holy Bible, is the exhibition of that
Divine compassion and desire, the working
out of that Divine purpose. It is that
Spirit which He brings into the souls of those
who are united to Him. The history of
the saints is the history of that Spirit striving
to realize itself in acts similar to His, in
the willing sacrifice of men seeking by all
means to bring back to the Father in Christ
those who were lost in misery and sin.
Therefore it is that Christianity is essentially
a missionary religion. It is impossible for
men to receive Christ into their souls and
not to receive that Spirit.

That Spirit is a world-wide all-embracing
Spirit. To Christ there are no bounds. To
speak of the Lord who stretched out His

arms upon the Cross as though He embraced
in those arms but a portion of the human
race is to destroy Christ.   It is to make Him
a local deity, or a mere human teacher, a
demigod, or a Jewish prophet.   If Christ
does not save the whole world He can save
none.   If my belief that Christ loved me
and died for me is not based upon the truth
that He loved the whole world and died for
the whole world, and that as I am a part of
the world, He loved me and died for me,
it is based upon a foundation of self-conceit
and vanity, upon racial or personal pride.
He whose Spirit cannot embrace all cannot
embrace any.   A limited Saviour is a contradiction in terms.   But if the Spirit of
Christ is all-embracing, the Spirit which we
receive is all-embracing ;   for we receive
Christ.   The Spirit given to us is the Spirit
of the command, and the command like the
Spirit is world-wide.

The Spirit which Christ imparts is the
Spirit of the command.   It is impossible for
men to be in communion with Christ, it is

impossible for Christ to dwell in their hearts by faith, and they not to have the Spirit which is the Spirit of the Incarnation. There dwells in them the Spirit Who led the Son of God to give up the very glory of Heaven in order to bring back the world to the Father in Himself. If Christ dwells in men, that Spirit dwells in them. If that Spirit is not in them, then Christ is not in them. There is no escape from this dilemma. If the Holy Spirit is given, a missionary Spirit is given.

How then does it come to pass that men who are communicants and otherwise devout members of the Church of Christ are yet sometimes open opponents of foreign missions? Surely this is only one aspect of a difficulty with which we are all most familiar. We are greatly tempted to deny the presence of the Spirit if we do not see those manifestations of the Spirit which our experience has taught us are proper and natural expressions of His nature. Other manifestations or manifestations which,

though of the same order as those which we
expect, are very slight, escape our observation.   At birth we expect a child to manifest
life, if he has it, in forms of expression which
our experience has taught us are common
and natural.   If we fail to see those signs of
life we may deny that the child is alive, and
yet a trained nurse or a doctor may be able
to discover signs of life, and with careful
nursing the child may grow up to healthy
manhood.   Possession of life and conscious
realization of the life and active manifestation of it are not identical.   So reception of
the Spirit and conscious realization of the
Spirit are not identical.   Reception of the
Spirit is a fact, realization and manifestation
of the Spirit is a process.

   This is why many are tempted to deny the
grace of sacraments.   We are taught that in
the sacraments the Holy Spirit is given.   Yet
the manifestations of the working of the
Holy Spirit may not follow as we expect,
Seeing this, men say " The grace is not given.
If the Spirit were there, the fruits of the

Spirit must appear." But the grace may be
quenched, or unnurtured. It may be neg-
lected, unrealized, unexercised, undeveloped.
Many children really alive perish for want
of proper observation and care.

Even in normal cases where a new-born
infant shows clearly the first signs of life
nurture and education are necessary. The
life so given left to itself could not survive
for more than a very short time. The child
must grow by degrees to learn the nature and
purpose and character of the life which it
possesses and of the environment in which it
is to exercise that life, so that it may attain
to full development, and may use its powers
for its own growth and not for its destruction.
Just so the newly baptized child has the
Holy Spirit, but it has little knowledge of
the nature of the Spirit. What is needed
is knowledge.

A gift of grace does not do away with the
need of knowledge. Grace received must
be recognized, known, accepted, surrendered
to, cultivated, proved by experience. We

must " know the things that are freely given to us by God." [1]   Christians are to grow in grace and in the knowledge of our Lord and Saviour Jesus Christ." [2]   The Ephesian Christians were " blessed with every spiritual blessing in the heavenly places in Christ," [3] yet they needed " a spirit of wisdom and revelation " [4] in the knowledge of Christ, that they might "know."   In the Church the exhortation to instruction follows immediately upon the administration of the sacrament of Baptism.

It is the work of the Holy Spirit to sanctify. There can be no hope of sanctification except as the consequence of receiving the Holy Spirit, yet it is necessary that those who receive the Holy Spirit should learn to know Him as a Spirit of Holiness indwelling them.   So the Holy Spirit is a missionary Spirit, yet it is necessary that those who receive Him should learn the meaning and power of the Spirit as missionary.   If the

[1] 1 Cor. ii. 2.   [2] 2 Pet. iii. 18.   [3] Eph. i. 3.
[4] Eph. i. 17–18.

Spirit is to be consciously manifested in missionary life, knowledge is necessary.

Now amongst us this knowledge is sadly lacking. We have all been taught that the Spirit of Christ is a Spirit of Holiness. We have all been taught to recognize the signs of His Presence in terms of virtuous conduct. We have not been taught that the Spirit of Christ is the Spirit which embraces the world and desires the salvation of all men. We have not been taught to recognize the signs of His Presence in ourselves in terms of missionary activity. Just so the Corinthians acquired a habit of recognizing the Spirit in terms of wisdom more easily than in terms of morality. But as it was bad for them to take a one-sided view of the Spirit, so it is bad for us. In the Church of England we have been taught from our infancy to believe in " God the Holy Ghost, who sanctifieth me and all the elect people of God." That, of course, does not exclude the truth that it was by the Holy Ghost that Christ was conceived of the Virgin

Mary. It does not exclude the truth that
He is the Spirit Who, proceeding from the
Father, sent the Son, and in the Son moved
Him to come into the world. It does not
exclude these truths ; but it has obscured
them. It has obscured them to such an ex-
tent that the vast mass of our people pass
from childhood to old age without ever
once having perceived them. What wonder,
then, that Christians who have been taught
a one-sided truth about the Holy Ghost
should be unconscious that they are denying
Him, when they deny that side of His nature
which they have never been taught !

Missionary zeal depends upon knowledge
of the Holy Spirit : it depends also upon
knowledge of the opportunity. Men on
this earth have been and must be limited by
their knowledge of the world and their power
of realizing the opportunities of their day.
There must be not only the presence of the
Spirit in the soul, there must be also a recognition of the heathen world, a realization of
the existence and the need of souls astray

from God to call that Spirit into action.
A man cannot possibly desire the salvation
of the tribes of Central Africa, if he does not
know that they exist.   In order to pity it is
necessary to know ; in order to work it is
necessary to know.

So far as the absence of missionary zeal
is due to ignorance of the world which
Christ embraces, all that is needed is informa-
tion.   For if the Spirit of Christ is in the soul,
the moment the existence of men without
Christ is revealed to the soul, that moment
the Spirit of Christ bursts forth in compassion and desire for them.   But where the
absence of missionary zeal is due not to this
ignorance, but to a restraint of the Spirit of
Christ, there is needed not merely informa-
tion, but spiritual renewal.   For here are
the signs of a most grave spiritual disease.

The restraint of the Spirit may be due
either to arrested development or to positive
rejection, deliberate refusal, open rebellion
against the Spirit.

There is such a thing as arrested development in the spiritual as in the physical world. Just as a child may grow normally for a time and then cease to make normal progress, so in the spiritual world the Spirit in men may be checked. Little children can at first manifest the Spirit of the Lord only in their own families or among their near friends. Then as they grow older and become aware of larger relationships, we expect them to be guided by the same Spirit in their dealings with school-fellows, masters, neighbours, fellow-countrymen. At each stage, as they realize the existence of the new groups, they ought to be governed in their conduct towards each by the same Spirit which governed their conduct towards the simpler groups. If, then, there comes a point at which this process is suddenly arrested, if they become conscious of a new group and the Spirit which has hitherto directed them fails to direct them in their attitude to the new group, there is manifest proof of serious spiritual disease. Suppose that a child grew straight till he was twelve or fourteen and then began to show signs of a weakening spine in bowed shoulders and narrow chest, we should call in a doctor. If a Christian as a child can desire the salvation of the members of his family, as a boy can desire the salvation of his own nation, but never arrives at the point when he can desire the salvation of the other nations, he needs a spiritual doctor. Yet as it sometimes happens that in certain ages and places bowed legs or backs or narrow chests have been treated with indifference, or have even become fashionable, so in our age spiritual dwarfishness has been a fashion. Men have not hesitated to boast that the redeeming Spirit of Christ in them is so weak that it cannot reach to China or to India. It is a strange thing that a man should be proud that he has not grown. If a Christian man has sufficient intellect to be able to apprehend the reality of the heathen world, yet has not sufficient spiritual charity to seek after the heathen in the Spirit of Christ, he is indeed a spiritual dwarf. St,

Paul prayed for his converts, that they might know the length and breadth and depth and height of the love of Christ. How shall a man grow up to such knowledge if his ideas of the length of the love of Christ cannot extend from Pentecost until to-day ? What can he know of the breadth of the love of Christ if it cannot reach to China or to South Africa ? What can he know of the depth of the love of Christ if it cannot move him with pity and compassion for the outcasts of India or for the tribes of the South Seas ? What can he know of the height of the love of Christ if he thinks that the Brahmin, the Buddhist, or the Confucianist is so advanced, so highly equipped, as to be beyond its scope. If to know the love of Christ is to grow up, a man who has no missionary zeal must be intellectually or spiritually " backward."

This is serious enough ; but the cause of the restraint may be even more serious. Just as men will sometimes surrender themselves to follow the guidance of the Holy Spirit in morals with a reservation, keeping in secret one precious vice which they cannot and will not give up, one point on which the Holy Spirit is refused a hearing, and His influence resisted ; so here a man may draw an arbitrary line, saying, " I will desire the salvation of my own family, I will desire the salvation of my own nation, but the salvation of such and such a people I will not desire." He may sincerely seek to be guided by the Holy Spirit in his dealings with his relations, his friends, his neighbours, and yet keep a limit beyond which he neither wishes nor intends to be guided by the Holy Spirit. Where this is done, there is a real denial of Christ. The only life of the soul is the Spirit of Christ. The Spirit of Christ reaches to those. Then in the Christian soul it must reach to those. If in the presence of those the love of Christ does not go out from the soul, it argues that the Spirit of Christ is hindered. Here is divided allegiance. How often have we been told the perils of divided allegiance !

If the Spirit which we receive, the Spirit of Christ, is thus a missionary Spirit, world-wide missionary zeal is something very different from zeal for a society. It is possible to have zeal for a missionary society yet no missionary zeal. Are there not clergy who, preferring a society to missionary zeal, have quenched missionary zeal in order to advance a society? Are there not laymen who have put their pet society into the first place, so that unless their missionary spirit could be expressed in and for that society it vanished? Such missionary zeal is not well founded. Sooner or later it will find a stronger basis on which to rest, or it will fall.

Missionary zeal is also something very different from an interest in Foreign Missions. Yet in our missionary work at home we have given the interest the first place. A few years ago the appeal took the form of rather lurid descriptions of the horrors which flourished under heathen religious sanction; to-day the tendency is rather to set forth glowing pictures of the wonderful results which we may expect to follow if we seize this or that moment or movement, and terrible pictures of the awful consequences which may follow if we fail in our duty. By these means we try to stir up interest in Foreign Missions.

These appeals may be compared to those which the Revivalists of the last century were wont to make. They tried to stir men to take an interest in their own salvation by vivid pictures of the delights of the redeemed, of the torments of the damned, with the reiterated " Now, Now is the day of salvation ; to-morrow it may be too late ; " just as we say " Now, Now ; in another moment the opportunity in Canada, or China, or India, or Africa will be gone."

Our appeals, like theirs, are based on profound and terrible truths ; but, like theirs, they are not based on proportion in the expression of the truths. Those terrible appeals of the Revivalist are seldom employed to-day. And for good reason. Such appeals are

dangerous. They are indirect appeals in
spite of their appearance of directness.
The Revivalist appeal was designed to make
men fly to the Saviour, moved by a paroxysm
of hope or fear. Beginning with one interest,
the preacher hoped to lead his hearers to
substitute another before the end. Terror
of hell does not necessarily lead to the
Saviour. It may lead away from Him.
So lurid accounts of heathen abominations,
glowing descriptions of wonderful opportunities, are indirect appeals. They may
lead to an outburst of compassion and desire,
or they may simply tickle the ears. Such
appeals moreover rouse an appetite that
grows by that it feeds on. The lurid pictures of hell became strangely attractive
to some who were least benefited by them.
So the eager appeals of missionaries have often
a strange attraction for some who take them
little to heart. And every time this sort of
appeal is made it must be made more vivid,
more striking, if it is to produce any effect
at all. The ear gets accustomed to a noise

which at first sounded horrible and does not notice it unless it is more violent than usual. So missionary books, even books for students, must be made more and more attractive, and their appeals to this peculiar type of interest more markedly emphasized. Even then there is always danger of reaction. Just as business men often go through their work under the stimulus of a foreign interest, doing things for which they care nothing, because doing them is the way to a living, and never learn to take any interest in the work in itself and for itself, and so the moment the stimulus is removed fly from the work, escape from the office with relief; so here, the moment the external interest in the thrilling appeal is removed, missionary work is left undone, because it never had any real interest of its own. Under the momentary stimulus of these appeals many take an interest in missions who know nothing of the missionary spirit.

Nevertheless, it is necessary to recognize that, just as the Revivalist appeals, so these

missionary appeals, have been widely successful.   We succeed beyond all that we
could ask or think because there are many
people in whom the Spirit of Christ is stirring, who are waiting for an opportunity to
express the Spirit.   All that they need is to
realize an opportunity, and they are ready to
seize it.   The Revivalist succeeded because
there were many souls in whom the Spirit
of Christ was stirring.   It needed only that
they should realize their need and His
grace, and they were ready to surrender to
the Spirit of Redeeming Love.   The fierce
assault of the preacher sufficed.   It opened
the door.

The success was unquestionable.   But
still the general tendency has been to refuse
such aids.   More and more we have seen the
dangers.   More and more we have seen that
the beneficial results which we at first supposed to spring directly from the sensational
appeal were really due not to the sensational
nature of the appeal, but to the fact that
some appeal was made which opened a door

for the Spirit. To-day in every other work
except alone the work of stirring interest in
missions we are shy of the sensational
appeal ; we rely more upon the education of
the soul, the quiet unfolding of the im-
plications of the indwelling Spirit. We avoid
dwelling too long on the foreign interest,
in order that we may make sure of the native.
And this is surely the right thing to do. The
"interest" which can be roused in most in-
quisitive minds in the nature of foreign lands,
the character of foreign peoples and foreign
customs and religions, is not necessarily
missionary at all. It may lead to missionary
interest, but it may fail. There is no question which is the interest that we need. It
is the interest of the Spirit of God in the souls
of men. It is the interest of Redeeming Love.
It is zeal.

Missionary zeal is grounded in the nature
and character of the Holy Ghost. It begins
with an act of reception. When men
open their hearts to Christ and He enters
in to dwell there, then enters the spirit of

missionary zeal. Missionary zeal is a form
of charity; and charity is not a gift of the
Spirit which one may have, another not have.
It begins in an act of reception, and it is to
be sustained not by renewed applications of
external stimuli, whether in the form of
orders, commands, or exciting stories and
appeals, but by repeated acts of reception,
repeated acts of surrender. The true missionary spirit is renewed not as much by
attendance at missionary meetings as by
attendance at the Holy Communion ; nevertheless by both.

(a) Missionary zeal thus depends upon
the state of the soul and its relationship to
God. Consequently it is wholly independent
of results. The Holy Spirit is not a Spirit
who lives upon outward success. The whole
history of the earthly life of our Lord illustrates that. Missionary work is the necessary
exercise of the Christian soul which can
realize itself is no other way. If all the
missions in the world were productive of no
visible results, the missionary spirit would

not be quenched. It could never be quenched
until the Spirit of Christ in the souls of His
people ceased to be the Spirit of Him who
came down into the world to save the world.

It does not follow that missionaries should
pay no heed to the results of their work.
Apparent failure should certainly lead us to
question whether we were manifesting the
Spirit of Christ in a right way. It is a dangerous delusion which persists in using
methods which apparently fail, on the plea
that we ought not to think of results. Such
a doctrine would justify the most stupid
methods. If we go forth in the Spirit we
ought to expect to see results. If we do not
see good results, our first duty is to question
our methods. To go on using methods
which do not produce good results is mis-
chievous, and to excuse ourselves on the
ground that the Spirit is more than method
is presumptuous. We are all familiar with
the preacher who excused his failure to
prepare his sermons by urging that God does
not need our learning. We have no right to

rest in manifest failure. As a matter of fact, we nearly always see the results of our work, and a little careful examination is generally sufficient to reveal the close connection between our methods and the results or want of results. To go on labouring without any apparent success may be the height of faith or the depth of stubborn self-will. To say that results do not lie in our hands may be a profound truth, but it may also be the folly of the wicked servant who buried his pound in the earth and expected his master to be satisfied with that action.

Apparent failure should make us revise our methods ; it ought not to make us deny the Spirit. To refuse to express our missionary zeal, because of apparent failure, would be to do this. In presence of apparent failure, the Christian soul must be unrestingly striving after some new form of manifestation by which it may succeed in revealing Christ to the world, and so may attain to that which it insatiably desires. The travail of the Son of God for the souls

of men is what it is, and manifests itself in
men as they are capable of manifesting it ;
but where it is it must manifest itself.

(*b*) Again, missionary zeal so grounded is
wholly independent of any doctrine of the
condition of the souls of heathen men after
death. Many men have been spurred to missionary labours by the belief that countless
souls of men every hour were passing to an
eternity of woe, and some men have argued
that the decay of that belief must result
in a decay of missionary fervour. But, in
fact, if that belief has perished, missionary
zeal has not perished with it. Missionary
zeal was never so sincere or widespread
amongst us as it is to-day. Missionary zeal
is not really dependent on any such doctrine.
Men ascribed their zeal to that because that
was the form in which they clothed their
sense of the need of men for Christ. We all
express ourselves in the terms familiar to us
in our own day. But spiritual realities do
not depend upon the form in which we express them. A crude doctrine of the Atone-

ment has not hindered men from receiving the benefit of the Atonement. A crude doctrine of the need of men does not affect the need. A crude conception of the working of the Spirit of Christ in the soul, which manifests itself in missionary zeal, does not affect the spiritual working. Our profiting by the work of Christ, our experience of the moving of the Spirit of Christ, is not affected by the mode in which we define or describe it. The missionary spirit is the Spirit of Christ in the soul, our missionary efforts are the manifestation of the Spirit of Christ in us ; our mental conceptions, our statements of the external impressions which seem to us to call that Spirit into action, may and do vary at different times and in different persons. To one this circumstance makes the most profound appeal, to another a different object seems all important, but in all it is the Spirit which is manifested, the Spirit of Christ the Redeemer, the Saviour.

(c) Similarly missionary zeal is wholly independent of our ideas as to the value or

character of heathen religions. To some
men it has seemed as if a belief that heathen
religions were wholly bad was essential to
any zeal for the spread of Christianity. The
more, they said, we tend to think that there
is much truth in heathen religions, the less
shall we feel the necessity of propagating the
Gospel. But this is not really the case. It
was to the people who had the best religion
known to the world that Christ first came.
He did not feel only the need of savages
for redemption. So Christians to-day are
not more zealous to preach the Gospel to
men whose religion is of the lowest type than
they are to preach the Gospel to men whose
religion is of the highest. Christians who
recognize much truth in heathen religions are
not less zealous in preaching Christ than
those who recognize little. Belief that the
religion of the heathen is bad is not the
motive which impels men to preach Christ ;
belief that the religion of the heathen has
much truth in it is not the motive. These
are only opinions which may change ; the

motive is the presence in the soul of the Redeeming Spirit of Christ, the Spirit which seeks to bring all men back to God in Christ. That motive does not change. Jesus Christ is the same yesterday, to-day and for ever.

(*d*) If missionary zeal is independent of our ideas of the value of heathen religious systems, it is also independent of our judgment of the moral state of those to whom we go. Men sometimes speak as though a conviction of the profound immorality of the heathen was necessary for missionary zeal. They sometimes speak as if moral heathen had no need of Christ. But Christ came first to the people who had the highest moral code, and probably the highest moral practice, known in the world at that time. And to-day Christians do not feel less anxiety to convert moral heathen than immoral. St. Paul was a highly moral Jew, but he did not therefore need Christ less than Zaccheus. People who think that that sort of morality affects the question of missions really themselves have not got beyond the stage of legal

religion. The question of importance is not
whether those to whom we go are more or less
moral, but whether they need Christ. The
motive which drives us to preach to them
is not a superior pride in our morality as
compared with theirs ; but the Spirit of
the Incarnation.

It is no doubt true that to many minds
the belief that the heathen who died
without hearing of the Saviour were lost
eternally, or that heathen religion and
heathen morality were devices of the devil
whereby he might more easily lead souls to
perdition by persuading them that they were
walking in the path of holiness, have been
strong reasons for earnest preaching of the
Gospel. But they were reasons, not motives.
They may be compared to the belief in the
speedy return of Christ, which in the early
days of Christianity was undoubtedly a
most powerful inducement to the Christians
to spread the Gospel because the time was
short. As time went on that reason and
these have all alike been modified. Doubt-

less as time goes on and knowledge increases we shall learn to modify many of our ideas, and our statements about truth. As we work, we shall learn sympathy with those to whom we seek to reveal the Lord, we shall learn more of the Truth itself, we shall learn to approach men more reasonably. But always, in all things, through all our strivings, and efforts, and methods, it is the same Spirit of the same Lord which cannot be restrained, embracing all men for whom He died, manifesting forth His grace in those whom He is pleased to call His missionaries, which is the fountain and source of all. The impulse is one, the motive is one : the forms in which the motive, the impulse, is expressed in men are many. The impulse, the power is Christ, Christ who embraces the world and gives us the world-wide command and dwells in us to fulfil the command.

THE HOPE

CHAPTER II

The Hope

THE Spirit which impels to missionary labour is the Spirit of Christ. All missionary desire and effort proceed from the presence of Christ in the souls of His people. He is the only source. He also is the end. From Him proceeds the impulse; in Him it finds its fulfilment; to Him it moves. The Hope set before us in the manifestation of Christ, the unfolding of His nature, the demonstration of His power, the revelation of His glory. Our Hope is Jesus Christ. We look for His appearing. We hope to see Him.

It seems to me to make a profound difference whether we accept this view of our work wholeheartedly. If it is important to know that missionary zeal is not something that proceeds from us, that it is not a natural gift, that though we can cultivate it we cannot create it, that it begins with an act of reception, and is an effect of the presence of Christ in the soul ; it is also important to know that the end towards which we strive is not a material, external result, but the unfolding of a Person.   A material result we may hope to produce or cause to be : the character, or nature, of the Person of Christ, though we may be agents of its manifestation, we cannot make.   We cannot cause it to be. This profoundly affects our whole attitude towards the forms and processes and methods of the manifestation.

We view them differently.   If interest in Foreign Missions can be internal, if, that is, it is the moving of the Spirit of Christ in us desiring the salvation of all men in Him ; or external, that is, having its source in the external processes by which our religion is diffused abroad ; similarly, as regards the end, interest in Foreign Missions may be internal, that is, it may be centred in Christ who is the internal reality, or external, that is, centred in the external results. A slave-driver takes an interest in the external results of the labour of his slaves : it is the result for which he really cares. A trader in feathers looks at a bird of paradise with an eye solely to the value of the feathers. A scientist looks at the feathers ; but he sees more than the feathers, he sees the bird. A friend or a lover may care very much for the actual results of the work or activity of his friend ; but it is the expression, the revelation, of the nature and character of the personality for which he cares most. In all the activity he never loses sight of the person. So we, if we seek a manifestation of Christ, may care very much for the external aspects of His revelation of Himself, but above all it is the revelation for which we seek.

We work differently. When we are simply working at the command of another, even though we may wholeheartedly accept the command, and most cordially approve the purpose of it, even though we may believe that the Author of the command is with us to help us in the performance of it, nay more, even if we believe that He is in us and works through us, yet if the end is perceived by us only as an external result, we seek to produce it; that is, we seek to produce that result.

But if we seek the manifestation of a Person, then that is impossible. We cannot then rest in an external result. If the manifestation of a Person is to be wrought out through us, if we are to take any part in it, we must subordinate ourselves definitely and closely to the Person whose manifestation we seek. Imagine a sculptor working under the direction of a master. Suppose he is given a design and told to block it out. He blocks it out. That is his task, to produce a given result which is plain and external. But suppose that the master sculptor for some reason would, or could, only work through his assistant in constructing and finishing his design. Then the assistant does not know exactly at the beginning of his work what the result will be. He only sees it as it grows under his hand and the hands of his fellow-workers. He is feeling for the unfolding of the master's mind. Such a one must be peculiarly subordinate to his master. He must not jump to conclusions. He must not seek to strike out in haste what he thinks would be best. He must not harbour strong prejudices as to the final result. If he seeks the revelation of the master's character and personality in the work, he must have his mind tuned to the master's mind. He must strive to express that rather than his own individuality. He must be peculiarly under the master's influence. His eye is rather upon the master than upon the work, or rather it is on the master in the work.

Of course men say that work done under these conditions cannot be the best work, that for the best work it is necessary that the actor should feel strongly the work done as his own, that he should be interested in the actual results produced above everything else, that he should express his own individuality in it as strongly as possible. Even when we do not definitely take that position, though we may sincerely believe that the hope before us is the revelation of Christ, yet, because we instinctively tend to dwell in the external, we are tempted to act exactly as those would act who set the results before themselves as the object to be attained and laboured to produce them first and last.

But this ends in weakness rather than in strength. Christ our Lord revealing Himself by the Holy Ghost is not like a human master impressing his own personality upon another to the other's annihilation. Only in Christ, only as filled with the Holy Spirit and in completest surrender to Him, do men really find themselves, and express themselves with truest freedom, and most complete power. When we realize most deeply that the work is not our own, that it is wholly beyond our power, that the results seen now are most glorious only when known as the manifestation of the will and character of Christ, then we most chiefly and truly delight in them because we really understand them, then we most certainly reach them because we do not misplace them, and then we do not fail by attempting what we can never of ourselves achieve.

We seek a revelation. A revelation is the unfolding of something that is, not the creation of something that is not. We are to have a part in the manifestation of the nature, the power, the grace of Christ, in the bringing back to the Father in Him of a world which has gone astray. But this is the unfolding of a mystery hid in God from all eternity, and complete from all eternity in Christ. In Christ the victory is already won ; in Him the Saints are perfected ; in Him the Church is complete. St. Paul told the Ephesian Christians that they were chosen in Christ before the foundation of the world. The New Jerusalem in St. John's vision came down out of heaven from God, it did not ascend up to God from earth. This divine mystery is the great reality behind the appearances of things. It is being unfolded. Thus we do not seek to make that to be which is not, we seek to bring to light that which is. It is in Christ. It is the Father's will to reveal it. What calmness, what security, what hope, is here!

We seek a revelation. A revelation is the unfolding of something which we do not yet see fully. It is being revealed. We do not yet see it. We do not yet see Christ. We see in part, in a glass darkly. We see with prophetic insight. Simeon saw in the Infant Christ a light to lighten the Gentiles; but he did not see the Gentiles enlightened. The magi saw the King; but they did not see Him reigning on the tree. The disciples saw Christ as they walked with Him during the three years of His earthly ministry; but they did not see Him as St. Paul saw Him when he wrote his epistles, or as St. John saw Him when he wrote the gospel. So we see Christ now. We see the Lamb of God; we see sin taken away by Him; but we do not see the sin of the world taken away. It is all about us everywhere. We

see the Prince of Peace ; but we do not see
His peace. The world is full of turmoil and
strife. We see the Lord of Truth, but we do
not see the Truth. We see rather a world led
astray by delusions. We do not see Christ.
We see but the fringe of the skirts of His
garments.

It is only as we see the fulfilment of His
work that we see Him. In Christ dwelleth
all the fullness of the Godhead. In Him all
things consist. He is the sum of all humanity. We may believe in that universality,
but we do not see it. Suppose we met a
man of whom it was said that he summed up
in himself all human speech. We might
accept that statement on the authority of
him who told it to us ; but we should not
know what it meant, still less what was
involved in it. We should only understand
it by watching the man as he went about the
world. Suppose then that we saw him
address a great crowd of men. Suppose
that we saw him hold their attention, excite
their imaginations, stir their passions, sway

their wills, carry them hither and thither
with his speech. "He can talk to these
people," we should say. "What people are
they?" "English." "Then he can speak
to the English." Suppose then that we
saw him again address another crowd, and
precisely the same thing happened. "He
can speak to these," we should say. "What
are these?" If the answer came back to us
"English," should we not at once turn round
upon ourselves and say, "We knew that
before. There is no new revelation here."
The impression of yesterday might be deep-
ened, but it would be the same. But suppose
we saw him address Russians, and Italians,
Turks, Afghans, Bengalis, Telugus, Tamils,
Burmese, Siamese, Chinese, Japanese, Coreans,
and all the tribes of Africa and of the islands
of the seas, and at every place the same thing
was repeated. All who would listen to him
were strangely and profoundly moved by his
speech. Just where the great gulfs in human
speech are deepest and widest, just where
one great family of languages ends and an-

other begins, just where all that we know
of grammar and sound fails us, where we
ourselves are most at a loss, where we find
that it is most difficult to pass, if there he
passed without any apparent difficulty at
all, just there we should stand amazed and
cry, " Now we begin to understand the power
of this man ! " And if we followed him
closely we might begin to say, " Now we
begin to understand something of his purpose
as well as of his power."

Just so it is with our knowledge of Christ.
We know that He can appeal to us. We know
that He can appeal to the Western peoples,
if they will listen to Him. We know something of His power, of His nature, of His
purpose. If we know any more to-day it is
because we have had Foreign Missions. We
ought to-day to have a clearer and fuller
conception of the nature and purpose of
Christ then our forefathers. We stand in a
better position than they stood in their life-
time. Yet how little we know ! How great
a glory lies before us ! There is here a pro-

found and strong incentive to missionary
zeal. We know enough to urge us to desire
to know more. We know enough to be able
to guess at a glory to be revealed. What
that glory will be we know not.

Here we touch the apologetic value of
Foreign Missions. The manifestation of the
universality of Christ, the fulfilment of His
claim to draw all men unto Himself is a
strong apology for our Faith. But, like all
true apology, it is much more than apology.
It is not mere defence of what is now held,
it is constructive advance into higher and
deeper visions of Christ. If the apologetic
value of Foreign Missions makes any appeal
to us, we speedily forget the apology in
the progress. To defend my faith is something; to find it, to enter into its triumph,
to know Christ and to be found in Him, to
see the dawning before my eyes of a new
understanding of His grace and power, is
something far more moving and inspiring.
It is the opening of the doors of the New
Jerusalem for me to peep inside and catch a

glimpse of the heaven of which the Lamb
is the light.

We seek a Revelation of Christ. A revelation is the unfolding of something which is,
not of something which is not. It is, therefore it will become. It is in Christ. Therefore our hope is certain ; for Christ is our
hope. It is certain in Him. But in us and
for us it is certain only in so far as we see it,
and enter into it, and experience it now.
There is a difference between Martha's " I
know that he will rise again at the last day "
and St. Paul's " When Christ, who is our
life, shall be manifested, then shall ye also
with Him be manifested in glory." The
one is a hope based upon a teaching; the
other is a hope based upon an experience.
The one is intelligent anticipation ; the other
is a foretaste, a present realization, an earnest
of the inheritance. Just as we hope for
that holiness without which no man shall
see the Lord, because we find in our hearts,
by the mercy of God, the presence of the
Spirit of Holiness, a Spirit striving, yearning,

urging us towards holiness—we have tasted
of the powers of the world to come : conscious of that, we hope ; so we hope for the
manifestation of Christ, for His appearance,
for the unfolding of the will of the Father in
the "dispensation of the fullness of the times
to sum up all things in Christ, the things in
the heavens and the things upon the earth " ;
because we see now, because we now find in
our souls a Spirit striving and yearning
towards that consummation, because now
we see a process going on before our very
eyes which carried on into the ages must
be so fulfilled. We taste of the powers of the
world to come, we see the first fruits, we
catch glimpses of the completion.   Thus
our hope is certain, entering within the veil.

We see this revelation in many forms.
I. We see it in the conversion of individuals,
in the influence of Christ over the lives
of individual men and women.   As we read
the Gospel stories of the healing of crippled
lives by the Divine Saviour, for a moment
we may be absorbed in the man upon whom

such a miracle of healing was wrought; we may forget for a moment the Healer in our wonder at the change which passed over the maimed life and brought it into freedom; but it is only for a moment. Presently there comes the vision of the Lord. Then it is the Lord who absorbs our whole attention. We forget to wonder at the cripple leaping and walking. The Lord, the Saviour, is revealed in him, and thereafter it is only with an effort that we bring back our minds to think about the change which came over the life of the man. Above all, and in all, it is the Revelation of Christ which chains our attention. This is as it should be. Herein lies one of the supreme glories of the Gospel narrative, an excellence often observed but seldom imitated. As we pass on down the path of history this light becomes more dim for most of us. St. Paul recounting the effect of his wonderful conversion on the Christians of his day could say, " They glorified God in me." But by degrees the history of the Church is written more and

F

more as the history of the people to whom Christ came rather than as the history of the coming of Christ to men.

To-day in our mission work we certainly allow ourselves to be absorbed too much in the story of the converts. We think almost entirely of the dangers and difficulties which beset them and of the hope which has entered into their lives. We allow ourselves to be detained too long by these considerations, because they are near to us and very real. Sometimes we speak too much of these and draw others to think over-much of them. We dwell so much on the outward life and circumstances, on the change as it affects the converts, that we are in danger of losing sight of the higher. Behind all this is Christ. And it is the revelation of Christ which is the real secret. Just as we now, looking back over the ages gone by, see the glory of Christ in the miracles of healing and in the miracles of conversion of the ancient world, so one day in the ages to come we shall see with a distinctness and all-absorb-

ing wonder, which to-day seems difficult,
the revelation of the Person of the Lord in
the conversions of to-day.

Even to-day we ought to make an effort
to see this, and to keep it before our minds.
It demands a real effort. Even in reading
missionary magazines we need to make this
effort. We find in these papers an extraor-
dinarily interesting collection of facts, and
stories, and statements, and theories;
but, unless we constantly recall ourselves, it
may escape our notice that we are really
reading papers which deal with the Revelation of Christ the Son of God. It seems
sometimes to have escaped the notice of the
editors and contributors. There is nothing
strange or surprising in that. It only
illustrates the pressure of the external.
It only brings home to us that if a man is
determined to make his hope the Revelation
of Christ, he must exercise some caution and
cherish that hope carefully in his bosom.
He must bring it to all missionary reports;
he must not expect to find it thrust upon

him. A hint here and there, a little encouragement by the way, is all that he should expect. If he finds those hints and encouragements, it will generally be because he brings the hope in his heart to his reading. Here as everywhere the more he brings the more he will find.

In the conversion of men we must persistently strive to keep Christ and His Revelation before us. To fail is not simply to suffer loss, it is to stand in real danger. If we allow ourselves in our missionary work to dwell too much on the human side, almost without knowing it men and men's souls occupy our whole horizon. The value of a human soul is so great that it is impossible to exaggerate it. Yet " Christ " is more than " Christians," and not " men " but " Christ " is our hope ; and the end for which we strive is not " men " but " Christ." " Converts " and " Christ " are not identical. Our minds habitually rest in one or the other term. It makes all the difference in which term they rest. If we habitually think and speak in the " convert " term, we tend to become individualists. Because the idea of the individual converts is stronger than the idea of the Christ, there is no effective unifying thought. If we habitually rest in the " Christ " term the unity is ever uppermost and prevents us from slipping into individualism.

If we habitually think and speak in the " convert " term we tend to think of numbers and to exaggerate the importance of numbers. " So many souls," we say, and " so many," " so many," is ever before our eyes. Then we begin to count (a practice which in the Old Testament was punished with a pestilence), and immediately we are in danger of wanting numbers so much that we tend to regard the means by which, and the manner in which they are made a little less. Or we tend the other way. We count and we draw a line. Whom shall I count ? We even pride ourselves upon the small number baptized. It is a sign of care. It argues a high standard. In either case the eye is on the converts all the time. But if we habitually rest in the " Christ " term numbers assume their proper place. The question which occupies the centre is not, How many? How few?; but Is Christ here being revealed? Can I find signs of Him? Numbers as " souls " do not cease to be important. There is no danger of careless indifference. We are more eager, not less. Yet the vice has gone out of numbers. The difference is startling.

The fact that we see these conversions wrought in different lands amongst peoples of very different habits of thought and life in widely divergent stages of civilization should help us to maintain a true attitude, and should bring home to us the truth with greater clearness ; because the mere fact of these differences forces upon our attention the grace and power of the Lord. We can hardly help looking beyond the convert in the case of a man between whom and ourselves there seems to be an almost impassable gulf. We sometimes hear people speak

as if the profound gulf which separates East
from West were a reason for refraining from
carrying the Gospel to the East. In truth it
is just that great gulf which should help us to
know what we are doing. Just as at home
it is the wide divergences between men
of different ages, between sexes, between
social position and intellectual education
which reveal to us the Divine humanity
of our Lord, because we see that all ages,
all sexes, all classes, all minds find in Him
their own proper development and completion, so that the child in Him becomes the
perfect child, the man the best man, the
woman the best woman, and the aged the
finest type of old age; so the profound dis-
tinctions which separate race from race only
minister to the revelation of Christ's universality. If the West finds in Christ its
ideal, so does the East. If Christ can attract
the Western mind and heart to Himself, so
He is seen to attract a mind and heart which
is most unlike, most unapproachable by the
Western mind. The more we emphasize the

gulf, the more we show, not that Christianity
is unsuited to the one because it is suited
to the other, but that the Christ is the Divine
Master who reconciles the irreconcilable.
That should help us to look beyond the converts, to see the Revelation of Christ in them.

II. We see the Revelation of Christ in
the growth and progress of the Church.
" To the principalities and powers in the
heavenly places," says St. Paul, is " made
known through the Church the manifold
wisdom of God according to the eternal
purpose which He purposed in Christ Jesus
our Lord." We cannot think of the Church
as an ark into which all kinds of beasts may
enter, but which remains the same whether
they enter or whether they remain outside.
The Body of the Lord makes increase and is
perfected ; the Temple of the Lord grows.
It is not possible to set Decorated windows
in an Early English Church, or to build
into it a Perpendicular chapel, without
affecting the whole character of the building.
Still less is it possible to bring into the Church

a Chinese, an African, or an Indian element
and not affect the whole. If in individual
enlightenment and restoration we see Christ,
how much more in the enlightenment and
perfection of the Body. Only in the last
few years have we begun to grasp at all
clearly what a world-wide communion
might mean. Already we are expecting
new ideas of virtue, new aspects of the
Truth of Christ. We begin to understand
what the foundation of native Churches in
China or in Japan, in India and in Africa
may mean for us all, bringing to us new
conceptions of the manifold working of the
Spirit of Christ. We begin to understand
that a world-wide communion does not
involve the destruction of local characteristics, that a world-wide communion is a
communion, a unity, catholic, apostolic,
not a loose federation of mutually suspicious
societies. This sense of the corporate unity
has come to us late, and we have scarcely
begun to see what it is; but we see that
it is the manifestation of Christ.

We see that the growth and progress of the Church is a manifestation of Christ ; yet we need to take pains to keep it clearly before our minds that the hope before us is not the perfecting of the Church, but the Revelation of Christ in the perfecting of the Church. It is only as a Revelation of Christ that the perfecting of the Church has any meaning. It is only as a result of the indwelling of the Holy Spirit of Christ that it can conceivably be attained. Nevertheless they are not the same. Christ is more than the Church. It is easy to put this on one side and to say that it is impossible to make the progress and extension of the Church our aim without making the Revelation of Christ our aim. But in fact they are not the same. If we cannot make even the conversion of men, the bringing of souls to Christ, our sole aim, without danger, still less can we make the extension of the Church our object without danger. It is possible to make the institution the end. But if it is dangerous to make souls of men our end, it is doubly dangerous to make an institution.

Interest in Foreign Missions is sometimes interest in the progress of a society, a missionary society, or a denomination, or a Catholic Church. There are appeals put forth for help in missionary work which suggest this, even if they do not openly proclaim it. Sometimes the appeal is even made for the strengthening, not of the Christian Church, but of the British Empire. It is an easy step. The Revelation of Christ is identified with, and subordinated to, the establishment and increase of the Catholic Church, then of that portion of the Church to which we belong, then of the society which appeals most to our own minds and affections, then of the Empire which in our minds is the strongest support of civilization and liberty. A worldly conception ends in a worldly campaign, a material conception in a material campaign. Our lust for statistics, our comparisons of added numbers, measuring ourselves by ourselves and com-

paring ourselves with ourselves, are all
the fruit of this worldly material conception.
There is a real gulf between seeking the
unfolding of a Person and the glorification
of a Society.

The Society is the Body of Christ, nevertheless it makes all the difference whether
we habitually think and speak of the Society
or of Christ. The one habit tends to make
us proselytize, to add numbers to our side
and to glory in the flesh of our converts.[1]
To induce a man to give up one religious
system in order that he may adopt another,
to abandon one religious society in order
to enter another, is not the preaching of
Christ ; it is Judaizing. But if our minds
habitually rest in Christ this is impossible.
We do not therefore think lightly of the
Body of Christ, because we see that Christ
is more than the Body. The only difference
is that if our minds rest in the idea of the
Church we can be absorbed in the external :
if our minds rest in Christ we cannot. In

[1] Gal. vi. 13.

the one case we can become partisans of
a limited and imperfect society, in the
other case we cannot. Yet men speak of
the extension of the Church as identical with
the Revelation of Christ. It is easy to say
that they are the same, because the manifestation of Christ is in and through the
perfecting of the Church. But it is not
reason thus to confound Christ with His
Church. Christ and the Church are not
convertible terms. It is not the same
thing to seek the manifestation of Christ
in the growth of the Church, and to seek
the growth of the Church. In the one case
" Christ," in the other " the Church "
occupies the centre of thought; and the
effect of that difference upon all missionary
work is most profound and far-reaching.

III. The Revelation of Christ in the
Church brings a revelation of Christ in the
world through the Church. We see not
only the establishment of the Church; we
see, too, the leavening of society. At home
and abroad society is more and more in-

fluenced by Christian ideals and principles. Non-Christian thought in India and China is becoming permeated with ideas which are essentially Christian. Christ is asserting His sway over those who do not acknowledge His divine authority. Can there be any good, any truth, any virtue outside Christ ? When Julian the Apostate urged a pagan world to fight the Christian faith by borrowing from the Christian armoury the weapons of charity, he was, in spite of himself, exalting Christ as King. When to-day we see the leaders of religious thought in India and Burma and China and Japan pursuing the same course, we see the world bowing before the Lord ; we see the manifestation of the glory of Christ ; we see the first streaks of light which hail a coming sunrise more glorious than we know.

All that is of truth in Eastern thought or teaching, all that is of virtue in heathen practice and life is of Christ and to Christ, and will find its fulfilment in Christ. Every step forward in social, moral, or intellectual

progress may be a revelation of Christ.
Yet here, too, it makes all the difference
whether we seek the manifestation of the
Person of Christ or the perfecting of social
conditions. The salvation of the nations,
the salving of the ship, is not the end.
The end is, that Christ may be all in all.
Christ is more than a Christianized world.
Just as we cannot arrive at Christ by adding
virtue to virtue, so we cannot arrive at
Christ by adding social betterment to social
betterment.

We see to-day the grave danger which
arises if we allow ourselves to dwell upon
the external conditions. There is a strong
tendency to-day towards propagating social
theories which seem to us Christian, towards
making the progress of the world our hope.
Men see the truth in heathen religions,
they see the virtues of heathen character
and they urge that the end of Christian
missionary work is not so much to convert
individuals, not so much to establish
the Church, as to leaven society and to help

forward a movement towards a goal of glory to which heathen truth and Christian truth alike are tending. They see this as the end, and their imaginations are fired by the vision of a world led by many paths to the throne of God. They sometimes talk as if the world were progressing naturally and by its own inherent character towards a fulfilment of perfection. Very often they speak as if the Christianizing of the world— that is, the leavening of human thought with Christian ideas—were the supreme end. The result is that they would make missionaries, preachers of social and political righteousness more than preachers of Christ.

It is easy to say that there is no difference, that there can be no progress without Christ, that all truth, all goodness, is of Christ, and that the preacher of social progress is necessarily a preacher of Christ. But if it is true that we can so set about the conversion of souls as to make men the end, if it is true that we can so set about the extension of the Church as to make the Church the

end, so it is equally, or, rather, it is doubly,
true that we can so set about the leavening
of society as to make the perfection of human
society the end. It all depends upon the
habitual resting-point of the soul. If we
habitually speak and think of the perfection
of the human race as the hope before us, we
inevitably tend to exaggerate the importance of local and imperfect theories of
social progress. We do worse than judaize,
we do worse than proselytize, we Westernize
in the most deadly and subtle way. The
introduction of purely Western theology
into our missions is bad, the introduction of
purely Western and modern sociology is far
worse; for then we overlay the Gospel instead
of preaching Christ. But if we habitually
speak and think of the Revelation of Christ
as the end, if it is the Person of Christ that
we desire above all things, we cannot rest
in social perfection, we cannot set a false
end before us, we cannot degenerate into
social reformers.

Our hope is Christ. In our missionary

G

work we expect a Revelation of Christ. Hence we cannot approach the heathen world as men who have nothing to gain, nothing to learn by our approach. We cannot speak as if all that we had to do was to bestow of our wealth, to show to others what we already perfectly enjoy, as though our salvation were complete without theirs. We cannot adopt an attitude born of spiritual pride and intellectual self-sufficiency. Our very compassion for those who know not Christ is mingled with desire and eager expectation. We without them are not made perfect. We without them may not see our Lord's glory. Christ is hidden there in heathen lands and we go to seek Him. In revealing Him to others we reveal Him to ourselves. We give not as a wealthy man may give to the poor of his abundance, that which he can spare without diminishing one particle of his own comfort; but as he gives who scatters his seed upon a rich field, looking for a harvest in which both he and those for whom he labours will find their life.

If the first contact with Christ is the reception of a missionary Spirit, the final hope set before us is dependent upon the expression and fulfilment of the work of that same Spirit. Hence Christianity is essentially a missionary religion. Its beginning is missionary; its end is missionary. What hope can he have who calls himself a Christian and is not missionary in heart and mind ? What new Jerusalem can he look for ? What revelation of Christ can he expect ? What salvation can he imagine ? How can a man who knows Christ say in his heart, "The revelation will come no doubt one day, but it is no business of mine " ? The only things that matter to us are the things that are ours. It is the idlest thing in the world to say, " I hoped for it, but I did not strive for it." In the last resort the only thing that matters to us is our own personal relation to Christ. If we look for a revelation of Christ the one thing that matters to us is what our relation to that revelation is when it comes. It may come as a revelation which is ours, because we, in very truth, have a part in it ; because when God made known to us the mystery of His Will—to sum up all things in Jesus Christ, we accepted that Will with joy and set our affections upon it and bent our wills to its fulfilment as the supreme object of our life.

THE MEANS

CHAPTER III

The Means

THE end is spiritual, the means also must be spiritual. The impulse is of Christ, the end is Christ, the means are in Christ. Christ is the source, the end, the worker. If it is true that we cannot even think of missionary work except as the Divine Missionary inspires us, it is also true that we cannot effect anything except as Christ uses us as agents for working out His purpose. All that we can do is to bring to Christ surrendered wills and heaits and minds to co-operate with Him. He is the only source of spiritual power. Missionary life begins with an act of reception; missionary zeal grows upon knowledge of the Spirit so received; missionary work is the expression of that Spirit in activity.

Such expression is necessary for us. We cannot possess a spirit without desiring to express it. We cannot feel love and hate and desire and compassion without seeking to manifest them. It is doubtful whether they can exist without any manifestation. What is love that is not an outgoing to somebody or something? It is certain that we cannot know them, it is doubly certain that we cannot increase in them, without expression. The spirit of holiness cannot survive except as expressed in holiness of life; the spirit of charity perishes if it is not exercised towards somebody or something. The very doctrine of the Holy Trinity is in some sense based upon this necessity which renders life without expression inconceivable to us. The Spirit must express, manifest, itself as light must shine.

Further, being constituted as we are, in a world constituted as this world is constituted, this expression must take material form. Here on earth spirit approaches spirit by means of material things, words and glances, and acts. All spiritual affections demand expression, and here we seek for a means of expression. We cannot feel love and hate and desire without seeking for some means to manifest our spiritual emotion. The woman in the Gospels could not be satisfied until her love for Christ had found expression in a box of ointment. So the Missionary Spirit of Christ in us cannot rest until it finds an expression in some form of sacrifice. We must give it form both for ourselves and for those to whom it is directed that it may become effective. Without this expression it is helpless, confined, perishing. It must find some outlet. It must clothe itself. This is why gifts of offerings are indispensable to the Christian soul.

Hence spring all the forms of missionary agency, societies with offices and clerks, money, books, schools, hospitals, churches, preaching rooms, orphanages, and every other kind of thing by which we strive to express our missionary spirit.

But it is the spirit, not these material things, which does the work. Just as the hope before us is not the external result which our labours may produce, so neither is the means by which we attain our end the material which we use for that purpose. We do not reach a manifestation of the Spirit without material things; but it is not the material which produces the manifestation. Our purpose is to reveal Christ to, and in, and through, human souls. But the moment we approach a human soul and attempt to influence it, we realize the impotence of material things. We cannot enlighten the eyes of a darkened soul by logical reasoning. "No man learns self discipline by hearing another man speak." We cannot reclaim a man from viciousness of life by eloquent speech. Habit holds him fast. We cannot bow a stubborn will with threats or promises. It is the heaven-born character of man that all the powers of earth cannot bend the will of a little child. Large salaries will not buy devotion. Costly education will not teach a lad to devote his life to Christ. No more can we convert the heathen by abundance of supplies or by the excellence of our organization, by money, or hospitals, or schools, or any other of these things. Only by spiritual means can spiritual results be produced.

Now, just as in speaking of the Hope before us we saw that it made a profound difference whether we habitually rested in the thought of the manifestation of Christ, or in the thought of the material, external form which that manifestation may take, so here it makes a profound difference whether we habitually rest in the thought of the expression of the Spirit or in the thought of the material form which the Spirit uses to manifest itself.

(*a*) It makes a great difference to us whether we constantly realize that it is the Spirit which is the effective force. We give money, we speak, we move about the world, we act in a very different way according as our minds habitually rest in this term or in that. In the one case we offer things, in the other we give ourselves. In the one case we measure our offerings by their material value, in the other we measure them by their internal value. In the one case we expect results to be attained by a false means, in the other by a true. In the one case we walk in the flesh, in the other we walk in the Spirit. In the one case we war after the flesh, in the other we war after the Spirit. In the one case we mind the things of the flesh, in the other case we mind the things of the Spirit. But that most seriously affects our life.

Are we then forbidden to deplore the smallness of the number of those who support missionary work, or to rejoice over an increasing subscription list ? Surely not. These things in this world are signs by which we may, nay must, diagnose the spiritual condition both of our own hearts and of the church of which we are members.

To think in the spiritual term is not to
deny that the Spirit is revealed in the form
and character of its expression. We deplore
a small meeting because it is a sign which
makes us fear a want of Spirit, we rejoice
over an increasing subscription list because it is a sign which makes us hope
that the Spirit is realized more fully. That
is a totally different thing from making the
external the end. We make the external
the governing factor when we despise small
meetings and small sums of money; when we
despair because boxes contain so little ;
when we threaten to give them up because
we can put little into them. We do so when
we think and speak as if God's work could
not be done without so much money or so
many men ; when we think or speak as if a
doubling of income necessarily involved
an increase of spiritual effectiveness, or as
if the admirable organization and equipment
of a station was our first if not our only
care. We must treat the external as the
servant, not as the master, but we do not

exalt the master by refusing to recognize the servant.

(*b*) It makes a great difference in our appeals to others. If we habitually realize that it is the Spirit which is the effective force, it is the Spirit for which we appeal. If what we want is Spirit, it is Spirit for which we shall ask. If we habitually think that material offerings are of no value whatever for our work, except as expressions of Spirit, we cannot possibly appeal for them as if they were of some value in themselves, apart from the Spirit which offers them. If our appeals are expressed in material terms, it is because we think materially.

Yet, because we are strongly tempted to dwell in the material, and to think that the material has in itself value for spiritual work, we often appeal for the material exactly as people engaged in purely secular work, like company promoters in fact, appeal in a frankly materialistic way; or sometimes, like tramps, we appeal to motives of all kinds, as though it really did not matter very much what motive was stirred so long as the material offering was produced.

We appeal for material as if it were the material that really mattered. The appeal for money can be made in a most material way. " Our ideal is to reach an income of £—— " " God's work cannot be done unless I get £——." The appeal for men is often couched in terms scarcely less material. How often do we read sentences like this : " The longer I am here, the more I am convinced that in . . . we . . . could win all along the line if only we had the men and the money " [1]? Appeals for men can be made, and are made, as though numbers really mattered in themselves. Even the appeal for prayers can be made singularly materialistic. How often do we hear appeals for " Chains of Prayer," or " All Day Intercessions," couched in terms which imply or suggest the idea that prayers can have an efficacy in themselves, which can be measured by their amount, just as coins can be calculated ? Prayers,

[1] *Q. I. P.*

as utterances, or as acts, are strictly material, and can be treated as materially as anything else. But it makes all the difference how we treat them, just as it makes all the difference how we treat money or men. That difference depends upon whether we habitually think and speak in terms of Spirit or in terms of matter.

Occasionally an attempt is made to justify this extreme insistence upon the importance of the material by arguing that, as we are dealing with Christians, we may take the Spirit for granted. All that is needed is to teach the right method of expression, and to urge the claims of the most important work upon the generosity of men who already know the generous impulse. We only need to turn the stream of generosity and activity into the right channel. It is more important that generous people should give their money for the conversion of the world to Christ than that they should give it to Homes for Cats or Dogs. We, therefore, appeal to them to give to the more important object.

To this it must be answered that what is
needed is not merely a change of form and a
change of method of expression, but a change
of Spirit. We often observe that the industry
and patience and ingenuity and perseverance
shown by criminals, if turned into some
useful channel, would suffice to produce
the most beneficial results both for themselves and for the community. But it
is not enough for the reformation of criminals
to point this out to them. The form of
their activity is the natural expression of
the spirit which they know in themselves.
To change the mode of their activity it is
necessary that they should know another
Spirit in themselves. They need to receive
that Spirit and to recognize its true character. Then their activity takes another
form. So it is, though in less marked degree,
with the generosity of many Christians.
If that stream of generosity is to be properly
devoted to some new form of activity, it is
necessary that they should know the Spirit
of Christ in them as a Spirit which approves

H

and desires that new activity. The old
motive does not suffice. The impulse which
urges them to this or that form of philan-
thropy cannot be changed simply by appeals
on behalf of a new form. The impulse must
be corrected. In other words, they must
get a new view of the nature and purpose
of the gift of the Holy Spirit. They must
receive the Spirit as a Missionary Spirit.
Then the new form of activity will be natural,
not forced; permanent not transitory. But
this result cannot be attained simply by
appeals for the material result. It can
only be effected by an appeal which touches
their souls. The appeal must be for the
Spirit rather than for the material.

The fact that grossly material appeals
do often touch the heart and produce great
spiritual results, is no reason for questioning this truth. It simply means that there
is something in the appeal which does call
up the Spirit, which does open the eyes
to that new view of the Spirit's mind and
purpose which is necessary. It is simply

an illustration of the fact that the Spirit transcends form, and can work in and through many forms which are not well designed. Behind these appeals there is most often a real devotion to Christ. The badness of the form in which it is expressed cannot destroy the Spirit. But neither can the devotion justify the badness of the form.

When we ask for these husks, we are in danger either of receiving the husks for which we ask, or of missing our object altogether. Generally, men's souls are not touched when we address their pockets. When we appeal to the Church for men and money as so much material, though the only thing that will really avail is the offering of souls, we translate spiritual things into material terms, and our material appeal loses its moral force. When we appeal not for souls of men but for their possessions, we use them as means to serve our ends. We want, I suppose, what we say we want; that is, something external to them, for an end external to them ; and men who have souls instinctively take up an attitude of reserve, of questioning. They feel that they are being exploited. They are not satisfied when they are told that our ideal is the doubling of the income of a society. They are not sure that missions prosper in proportion to their wealth. They have a dim feeling unexpressed that the whole subject is being put on an improper basis.

(c) Furthermore, it makes a great difference to those to whom we send our missions whether we realize that the Spirit is the effective force and habitually act and speak in terms of the Spirit rather than of the flesh. Men instinctively reach out to find the Spirit which actuates the words and actions of those with whom they come in contact. One of the missioners who went in the Mission of Help to South Africa a few years ago was met on the threshold of his work with the remark, " If people feel that you have no ulterior motive in coming here they will be so surprised that you will have

a great response." It is the motive, the
Spirit, which influences men's souls. We
send men, we build hospitals, and schools
and churches. The people look at them
and seek to find the motive at the back of
them. At first, heathen men naturally
ascribe to the authors of these things some
motive with which they are familiar. But
sooner or later they will find out the real
motive; for it is the real motive which
abides and works, and in the end emerges.
Then it is of infinite importance that
there should be a strong spiritual force
behind the works. That is why it is true
that in missionary work everything depends
upon the spiritual state of the Church which
sends the mission. It is not only the Spirit
of the men sent which counts. The Spirit
behind the mission is not only their Spirit,
it is the Spirit of the Church which sends
and equips them.

Yet we hear appeals for missionary work
based upon fear of disaster, political or social;
upon desire for the security or progress of

the Empire; even upon the hope of com-
mercial advantage.   We have been invited
to ward off the perils of materialism in
China or in South America by the most
material appeals.   Happily, such appeals
fail in most cases.   If our missions were
really founded upon such motives, sooner
or later those to whom we send our missions
would discover them.   Would our missions
then reveal Christ ?   Such motives, I imagine, we should wish to keep concealed from
the heathen world;   we certainly should
not expect any one to be converted by them.
But if behind our missions is the Spirit of
the Redeemer, if that is the Spirit upon
which they are founded and from which
they spring, then when the heathen discover
the real motive behind the works, they are
face to face with the Holy Spirit of Christ,
of God.   There is power for the Revelation
of Christ, there is power for conversion,
there is the means by which the Hope of the
world may be fulfilled.

This is why every Christian man ought

to feel that he can only attain his Hope by
the fullest possible expression of the Divine
Spirit of Christ given to him, to indwell
him, to work through him. He must express
the Spirit of Christ and no other, and no
other man can express that Spirit for him.

When we think in this way we can scarcely
be surprised that our missions have not
made greater progress.

Giving is not the easy matter which we
sometimes fancy it to be. If we give without
careful attention to the manner of our giving
we should not be surprised if the result that
we attain is disappointing. If we give as
we should give to beggars, casting an easy
dole to them, we ought not to be surprised
if only beggars accept our dole, or if nobler
souls perceiving the infinite value of that
which we give so lightly, receive it without
feeling any very deep gratitude to us. We
ought to be at least as careful in our giving
of the Gospel to the civilized people of the
East as we should be in giving presents to
our friends, lest haply in our manner of

giving we may hurt their feelings, and irritate them rather than attract them. In all giving it is the motive which suggests and directs the giving which is of the first importance. If we give from material motives in response to a material appeal we should not be surprised if we make " rice Christians." It is wonderful how few " rice Christians " we have made. The taunt of " rice Christians " is out of date, put to shame by the light of facts, in the mission field ; but its real sting is at home. It forces us to question whether in our giving we have not deserved " rice Christians." When we think of the nature of the appeals constantly made to us and of our response to them, we may well be filled with gratitude and thankfulness that our failings have been forgiven and our efforts blessed above all that we could have hoped or have dared to ask.

Only by spiritual means can spiritual results be effected. But the Spirit works through the material. Even so it was the Lord of Glory manifested Himself. He

took a material body and so fulfilled it with
His Spirit that it became to all ages and to all
the world the manifestation of the Godhead
which no man hath seen nor can see. So
it was that He instituted a religion of sacraments. There is in Christ no ignoring of
the outward material form. The whole
world is sacramental and Christ is sacramental and the religion of Christ is sacramental, because He is sacramental.

Because Christ is sacramental missions
are sacramental. We act as Christ acted.
His Spirit works in us and manifests Himself
in us as He manifested Himself in His own
Body.

This is the power which God has given
us, the power of making material things
into the vehicles of spiritual force. We
see this every day. We see men take some
material thing, it matters not what, and
use it as the vehicle by which they express
their souls. A lover takes a flower or a
piece of metal and so infuses it with his
desires and longings and hopes that it becomes

a thing of power. It conveys a meaning, a power, which is not its own. It retains its own character as a material thing, but it receives a new character as a love token. It is more than itself; it is a sacrament. Just so the missionary spirit which Christ brings into our souls seizes upon money, and bricks and mortar, and paper and ink, and all manner of things, and gives to them a new character, a spiritual character, and makes them the instruments of spiritual force.

This spiritual force is boundless in its working.

(a) It is not confined by limitations of time or space. The Spirit gives something of spiritual liberty to the material. The widow who offered her two mites at the Temple did this. She desired to express a spiritual emotion. She seized upon the only material vehicle at hand, she made that the instrument by which she could express her spirit. She became a fellow-worker with Christ. Christ saw in her offering a spiritual act. He blessed it.

The widow is dead and buried, and no man knows who or what she was. Two thousand years have passed away, yet the spiritual force expressed in those two mites is working in the world in an ever-widening circle. It exercises an influence far greater to-day than a thousand years ago. A thousand years hence it will exercise an influence far greater than it does to-day. The spiritual force with which these two mites were endowed has caused them to pass out of the dominion of time and space. They live and work still as a means by which a Spirit revealed itself and was accepted and blessed by the Lord. Without them that Spirit could not have effected its object. Filled with that Spirit they transcend all limitations.

So it is with the spiritual offerings of all God's children. The material in which the Spirit clothes itself appears to be mean and small and bound by countless bonds. We put a coin into a box and think of it too often as a mere piece of metal. It need not be, it should not be, a mere piece of metal. A mere piece of metal cannot effect any spiritual work. It is bound by all the limitations of the world. But filled with the Spirit it overleaps all those limitations. As vehicles of Divine compassion and desire, pieces of metal do convert the world, do bring the Gospel of our Lord to heathen souls, do build up a spiritual temple, do bring near a Revelation of Jesus Christ. They work in China, or in India, or in the islands of the sea, in the furthest bounds of the globe. Whither the Spirit is to go they go, what the Spirit is to work they work, for the Spirit of the Lord is upon them.

(b) The spiritual force transcends material weights and measures. It is not bound by the limitations of its instruments. We recognize this in our common dealing with material things. The gifts which we offer one to another have two values, a value in the market, and a value as an offering of affection. The market value is the value which the instrument which we use has in itself before it is clothed with spiritual grace. Its value as an offering is the value which it has as clothed with that spiritual grace; it is the value of the spiritual grace with which it is clothed. The value of the box of spikenard with which the woman anointed the feet of the Lord was great materially and spiritually. The value of the widow's mites was small materially, but great spiritually. The spiritual power was not affected in either case by the material value of its instrument. Hence the peculiar preciousness which often abides with little offerings of affection which in the market are quite valueless.

But whilst almost any material thing, however poor in itself, can be made the instrument by which the Spirit works, the Spirit ever seeks the best possible vehicle for its manifestation. The Spirit of the Lord is shown in the Incarnation and the Passion. The widow in the Gospel story had two mites; she gave her all. The woman who offered ointment, offered costly ointment. Great desires, great affections seek an adequate expression. A great love sacrifices much. A great desire spends much in the pursuit of its object. We can no more express great desires, great affections, without costly sacrifices than we can change the meanness of our souls by mere costliness. The form which our offering takes is the measure of our judgment : the costliness of it in money, or in care, or in thought, or in labour, is the measure of our desire. Wholehearted devotion is satisfied only when it is expressed in complete and entire self-sacrifice.

We sometimes delude ourselves in this matter. We imagine that our devotion is greater than its expression. We imagine that our devotion is great when our offering is small. We imagine that we can excuse or atone for the refusal of personal service by payments of money. We imagine that we can condone small offerings by adding an apology. Things which we do with an apology are things which we have never taken seriously. An apology is either a defence, or a confession of failure with an implied or expressed promise of amendment. It cannot be an excuse, still less can it add any virtue to an action. Our offerings are chosen by us because they express our spiritual attitude. They are the natural clothing which the Spirit elects to use. They represent with singular accuracy our attitude to the person or object to which they are made. If they are mean, it is because the mean spirit naturally expresses itself in a mean form. The liberal deviseth liberal things. He cannot help it. And the missionary-hearted gives his best to missions because he is missionary-hearted. He cannot help it.

(c) The spiritual force of an act of devotion transcends not only the limitations of time and space, not only material standards of value, but also the nature and form of its expression. The goodness of the form is a matter of judgment; the outpouring of the Spirit is a matter of devotion. The devotion of the soul is not for the form of its expression, but for its object. It is quite open to question whether the widow in the Gospel found the best possible form of expression when she gave all her living to support a temple which our Lord described as a den of robbers. When the disciples murmured at the woman in Bethany, that she lacked judgment in her mode of expressing devotion, Christ did not answer that she had chosen the best form. He answered that she had used the only means possible to her, that she had done the best she could. He blessed both these acts, and the whole Church to-day is inspired by the sacrifice of the one and moved to devotion by the other. The spiritual force was there, and with Christ's blessing it was not hindered from attaining its object by any possible criticism of its form or method.

So it is with us. Men criticize the form and method which we employ to convert the heathen and to reveal Christ, and often we ourselves criticize them. Sometimes under the influence of this criticism we are tempted to hold our hands. Men to-day are often tempted to refuse to allow the missionary Spirit of Christ in them to find its proper effective exercise because the Church is not her own missionary society, or because of some criticism which is passed upon missionaries or upon missionary societies. Then it is that we need to remember that the Spirit transcends the form. Because we cannot find the perfect, the ideal form of expression, shall we therefore make no offering at all ? If we desire to obtain we shall use, we must use, the best method that we can find to attain our object. We cannot possibly refrain from using it. It is better to use a bad form of expression than none. It is essential to the life of the soul to find some expression. We stifle the Spirit of the Lord within us if we refuse every expression because none is quite ideal. So long as we are on this earth every form of expression that we can find will lie open to some criticism; because there cannot be a perfect method in an imperfect world. The best we can find is all we need in order to express our longing and desire for Christ. What we can is all that He asks. The Spirit is not hindered by the imperfection of its method of expression. The work of the Spirit is wronght by the Spirit not by the form. It is wrought in and through the form, but the form is subject to the Spirit, not the Spirit to the form.

The method is subject to the Spirit, not the Spirit to the method. Nevertheless, the Spirit cannot be satisfied with any but the best methods. Just as the Spirit is not hampered by the smallness of the means at its command, but cannot use less than the whole of the means ; so it is not hampered by the weakness of its method, while yet it cannot employ any but the best possible method. We cannot possibly despise the outward form, or treat it as if it could be thought of as independent of the Spirit of which it is the embodiment. One mite cannot be made the instrument of a Spirit which possesses two mites. A small mission cannot be made the instrument of a Spirit which can procure and can fill a large mission. An ill-organized, ill-directed school cannot be made the instrument of a Spirit which can command a well-directed school. The Spirit cannot express itself, cannot do its work with less than its best material, its best form.

Hence the souls of men as they grow in the knowledge and power of the Spirit of Christ must be ever seeking larger and finer methods of expression, constantly calling for larger and purer sacrifice in order to reveal that Spirit to the world and to accomplish His purpose. We cannot stand still. We are sometimes tempted to be impatient of criticism, and to resent the demand for better methods. " Give us men and money," we say, not " methods." " It is personality alone that matters. What we want is the Spirit. Men who have the Spirit can use any method. Let us cease from all this talk about organization and method."

So far as this attitude represents a recoil from a materialistic view of our means and an assertion of the supremacy of Spirit in spiritual work, we must sympathize with it. It is the Spirit that matters. God has chosen the weak things of the earth to confound the mighty. He does not need large supplies. Christ could feed 5,000 men with five loaves as well as with 200 pennyworth of bread. Prayer offered in the Spirit is not ineffectual because the form in which it is expressed is ill conceived. A preacher full of the Spirit of Christ can reach his hearers' souls in spite of a stammering tongue. Great missionaries triumph over the limitations of their methods and equipment. The methods of the greatest missionaries may be criticized : their success cannot be gainsaid. There is no doubt that the Spirit transcends the form of its expression.

On the other hand, so far as the attitude implies the assumption that spiritual persons can afford to ignore the nature of the form in which they express their spiritual devotion, it is false. Spirit transcends form and matter, but it is not satisfied with less than the best obtainable offering. Christ could feed 5,000 men without 200 pennyworth of bread, but He demanded all that the Apostles had. They had five loaves, and they gave them all. Christ asks of us what we can. It does not suffice to give Him a part, and to plead that if we do not keep back part we shall not have enough for our own consumption. Similarly in respect of methods. The best method is not enough; no method is sufficient; but none but the best possible method is good enough. Refusal to study the best methods, refusal to regard organization as of any importance, is really not the denial of matter, but the denial of the Spirit. It is sloth, not faith. We ought not to treat the external form as something to be despised as a sort of accessory of spiritual life. It is in truth the very body of the Spirit without which the Spirit is unclothed and impotent. The most spiritual sacrifice is not a sacrifice without any visible offering, but the most spiritual offering of the material sacrifice. So it was with our Lord, so it is with us. As His spiritual offering was the offering of a Body, so our spiritual offering is the offering of ourselves, all that we are and all that we have, body and soul, affections and possessions. So clothed, the Spirit of Christ can work out through us that for which the Spirit is given to us, the Revelation of Christ to the world.

THE REACTION

CHAPTER IV

The Reaction

IN the preceding chapters I have tried to show that the source of all missionary zeal is the presence of Christ in the soul. Missionary life begins with an act of reception and grows by an advancing knowledge of the Spirit so received as a world-wide all-embracing Spirit. The end of all missionary desire is a Revelation of Christ, a world-wide Revelation, a more than world-wide Revelation. The means by which we attain is the strongest possible expression of that Spirit in outward form over the widest possible field.

But these things are not generally realized. It is sadly true that, in the Church at home, many who recognize the Holy Spirit as the Spirit of Holiness fail to recognize Him as the

Spirit of Missions; that many who recognize Him as the Spirit of Charity, even of missionary charity, fail to recognize the essential and profound reality of that which they avow. Charity is one of the fruits of the Spirit, but it is more than one of the fruits of the Spirit ; it is the Nature of God.   Missionary charity is one of the manifestations of Charity, but it is more than one of the manifestations of Charity : it is the expression of the Nature of God in relation to this world.

It makes some difference whether we look upon the support of missions as one amongst many manifestations of a Spirit of Charity, whether we look upon Charity itself as one amongst many fruits of the Spirit, or whether we look upon Charity as the Nature of the Spirit and missionary charity as the manifestation of that Spirit in a world which needs above all things Redeeming Love.   And it makes some difference whether we look upon Redeeming Love as active *towards* us only, or as active in us towards others; whether we receive a Spirit of Redeeming Love

embracing the world which is active in us, and
proceeds from us, or a Spirit of Redeeming
Love which proceeds from God to us and
stops there.

This is a matter of vital importance, not
only because it enables us to support missions
properly, but also because it intimately
touches our own life. What we need to be
assured of is not that we possess an excellent
system of doctrine and ritual, but that the
gift of the Holy Ghost is a reality. If then
we find in our own souls a Spirit which desires,
and longs for, and works for, the bringing
back of the whole world to God in Christ,
we are compelled to recognize in the most
vivid and definite way the fact that the Spirit
of Christ dwells in us. For that Spirit which
so desires the salvation of the world, the
Revelation of Christ is not a natural thing.
It is not born in men by nature. The natural
man does not desire the Revelation of Christ
to the world and in the world. He may desire progress, but not Christ. The desire for
Christ, the desire of Christ in the soul, is a

certain sign of the presence of the Spirit of Christ. If then a man finds this in his own soul, he is convinced of the reality of the Holy Spirit's indwelling in his own soul. Humbly to recognize that reality is a step of the most momentous importance in the life of the soul. It means that men step out of dim hopes into certainties and realities, out of hazy notions that in some way Christ helps them, into certain consciousness of His life in them. Thankfully recognized and accepted, that leads them into a new life and liberty which cannot but alter their whole influence upon all around them. They do more than support missions abroad; they become and are different men at home.

When we know that we receive such a Spirit, a Spirit which goes out to the uttermost bounds, our whole heart and mind is uplifted and enlarged That cannot affect only our attitude to men in distant lands, it affects also our attitude to our next-door neighbour. The sympathy that can feel for Zulus or Japanese can feel the needs which lie

close at hand. It is not the perception of
this Spirit which makes men anxious to
propagate the Gospel abroad and careless of
the condition of people at home. When that
occurs, it is due not to the perception of the
Nature of the Spirit, but to want of perception.
People do sometimes try to escape from the
commonplace home duties by launching out
into what seem to them great and glorious
schemes for the amelioration of the lot of
people whom they have never seen ; but
that is not the expression of the Holy Spirit,
but of a spirit of restlessness and discontent.
The Spirit which embraces all, embraces all,
not some, neither some here nor some there, but
all both here and there. To know the Spirit as
a Redeeming Spirit, embracing all, is to know
the Spirit as a Spirit of active redemption
both to these and those. And in fact is it not
much more common to find the restraint of the
Spirit on that side rather than on this ? Is it
not much more easy and more general to live
in our own things than in the things of others?
The remedy for both faults is not to restrain

the Spirit, but to receive more fully of the Spirit. A conviction of the power of the Holy Ghost which is sufficient to carry a man over every barrier of time and space, every gulf intellectual, moral, spiritual, and social, is sufficient to enable him to face hopefully and helpfully the difficulties of his own people.

This is surely not far removed from the fundamental principle which underlies the assertion that we ought never to rest satisfied with the support of local and particular missions abroad, still less with the support of individuals. What our souls need is to know the Spirit which is given to us of God. That Spirit is all embracing. It may be a stage in our education to carry our interest to some one point, or to some one person, outside our own immediate circle; but that is still infinitely far from a perception which is easily within our grasp. If people rest in such a little advance they easily slip back, as may be seen every day. With the removal of the temporary and local interest their zeal disappears. The care for some particular and local mission or missionary, or detail of a mission, is not in itself any security that the principle has been grasped, or the truth really seen, and it is this which is the matter of vital importance.

The apprehension of this truth makes real to us our relation to Christ as the Redeemer. It also makes clear to us our relation to the Church. In the past we have failed largely because we looked upon the Church of England as a Church for England. We thought that all that the Church had to do was to feed English Christians, and all that English Christians had to do was to be fed. The result was inertia, sloth, degradation. We have come to be almost thankful for attacks upon the Church at home. Attacks upon Church schools and Church endowments do not seem wholly evil. They stir us up. They rouse the Spirit of Churchmen. They compel men to "take an interest" in their Church. How desperate and ignoble that is!

When once a man has admitted the all-embracing Spirit of Redeeming Love he can no longer look upon the Church as an institution designed to supply certain spiritual and social needs of the people here. He is delivered from the twin demons of parochialism and pauperism. If even to-day vast multitudes of people who call themselves Christians and Churchmen live as though the Church was their nursing mother and they babies, it is not the missionary-hearted who are of that number. If to-day vast numbers of people who think themselves Christians and Church-men have to be goaded and driven into taking any thought or care for the Church as a whole, or even as represented by their diocese, it is not the missionary-hearted who so fail. The moment that we recognize the Spirit in us as a Spirit of missions, we know that we are not partakers of Christ for ourselves alone, we know that the Church which does not conquer the world dies. To luxuriate in the rich pastures provided for us largely by the zeal of men in years gone by becomes an absurdity, a denial of the life, a denial of the grace given to us.

But the apprehension of the Spirit of Christ as a missionary Spirit not only drives us out of pauperism and parochialism ; it also drives us to look beyond the bounds of our own Communion. That missions abroad have forced us to consider the great dangers of our unhappy divisions in an entirely new light, and have brought home to us their wickedness with new force, is unquestioned.

The cause of this is not simply that " the time is limited. For the accomplishment of our overwhelming task, it seems essential that the Christian Church should present a united front. The issues are so great that there can be no trifling in the matter." [1] That is the form in which the movement towards unity is generally expressed. But it is not, I believe, really the greatness of the issues which is driving us towards unity. No one can study our Foreign Missions with-

[1] *Report of the Commission on Co-operation and Unity of the Edinburgh Conference.*

out realizing that there is truth in the statement.   The issues are so great that anything
which hampers us in our labours seems a
crime.   But that is not the foundation of the
movement.   The foundation lies in some
deeper source than in the pressure of any
outward   circumstances   however   great.
Events which have illustrated the movement
towards unity within the Church itself, and
as it affects different denominations, have
been the Pan-Anglican Conference, the Edinburgh Conference and the recent Conferences
held in different parts of the East under the
Presidency of Dr. Mott.   But at the Pan-
Anglican Conference, at Edinburgh, and at
Calcutta, the witness of those present was
not so much that they were impressed with
the truth that it was " essential that the
Christian Church should present a united
front," as that there was an extraordinary
feeling of unity and harmony present then
and there.   It was the same at Edinburgh,
and the same at Calcutta.   Christians met
and felt not simply that they must find a

way out of their divisions, but that they were much more united than they expected.

In the *International Review of Missions* for April, 1913, there are three papers upon the Conferences held in India under the Presidency of Dr. Mott. In every one this fact is noticed. " The frankness of the discussions astonished many, and, above all, the fact that such frankness could co-exist with such complete unity of spirit," says Mr. Farquhar. The Bishop of Madras thought that " it would have been difficult for any outsider, who might have come into the Conference without knowing its composition, to have guessed that it brought together the representatives of different denominations supposed to be antagonistic. Throughout all our work and discussions there was the deep underlying sense of a great common cause that united us all in the bonds of brotherhood. There was no effort needed to sink our differences. They did not emerge on the surface." " Those who come together," Mr. Maclean observes, " though belonging to many countries and differing widely in their views of doctrine and polity as well as in opinion regarding the problems under discussion, were conscious of a strange oneness."

This strange oneness, this surprising discovery that though we are not agreed we are united, was the result, the inevitable result, of the mutual recognition of redeeming love in one another. The moment missionary-hearted people meet with any degree of intimacy, the Spirit in one recognizes the Spirit in the other, and bursts through all barriers of custom and habit of thought to greet the other. The pressure of circumstances, a sense of the importance of the issues at stake, perhaps first brought them together, but that did not unite them. This union was something that they discovered, not something that they made.

This union which they discovered was internal, spiritual, essential, lying far below the surface of things, obscured by many differences and disagreements, but of the most profound reality, because it was Christ. The moment that men acknowledge that their neighbours are united to Christ, to whom they themselves are united, they cannot deny this real unity. Consequently the realization of the Spirit of Christ in ourselves and in others is the first step towards external unity. It is this that we see becoming more and more a powerful influence in missionary experience. It is to this that we look with confidence. The pressure of external circumstances may pass away. A unity which sprang out of that sense of pressure would then disappear and elements which had been forced by that pressure into temporary agreement would again fly apart. But this vital underlying unity in the Spirit grows with the growth of the members who realize it the more, the more they know what Spirit they are of. In unity they find themselves: in accommodations forced upon them by the pressure of circumstances they rather suppress themselves in order to maintain an external appearance of unity. The vital unity recognized must issue eventually in agreement, an agreement not necessarily of uniformity, but quite reasonably of diversity. It is in this way that missions make for unity, and it is in this way, I believe, unity will be attained. It will be by discovery not by creation. The discovery has begun to be made.   The more it is discovered the more it will find expression in harmony of feeling, of mind, and of will.

II. A true apprehension of the Hope set before us does not merely enable us to carry on our missionary work truly and rightly, it also exercises a most important influence now at home. It affects our own spiritual life, it makes the meaning and purpose of the gift of the Holy Spirit real to us. It carries us out of the land of vague aspiration along the path of intelligent effort. The hope set before us as Christians is apt to be for many of us peculiarly vague. We have no precise or clear notion what we ought to expect in the future either as regards the life of the individual soul, or as regards the common, general, final end. This vagueness is, I think, very common and very distressing to large numbers of Christian people. The moment we see the consummation of the age, the completion of the Church, the adorning of the Bride, the summing up of all things in Jesus Christ, not simply as terms which dimly set forth a kind of general perfection, but as the conclusion of a process which here and now before our very eyes is appearing with all that definiteness and clearness of outline which belongs to things with which we are quite familiar, so that we have only to imagine the process which we see now quite distinctly going on to its fulfilment, it may be for a short time, it may be for a long time—short and long being merely terms which vary for us from day to day—the end expressed in those vague terms immediately assumes an extraordinary reality.

The apprehension of this reality has not merely an intellectual, but also a moral value. When we see these things clearly they not only satisfy our minds, they stir our hearts, they strengthen our wills. Vagueness as to the end inevitably results in weakness of intention and feebleness of effort. No one does really good work when he is not quite sure what he is driving at, or when the end before him is so far distant and ill distinguished that he really cannot make it out clearly at all. An apprehension of the hope set before us is an apprehension of something which we *are* attaining, not of something that we may at some time attain. This makes a most profound difference to our moral life. This is the kind of hope which makes martyrs, and strenuous workers, and cheerful and contented people. This kind of hope irradiates the life of every day, and enables people to face disappointments, discouragements and failings, even their own failings, with a quiet confidence of final success.

This influence of the missionary hope, coming with such moral force and power, uplifting the whole man and his life, cannot possibly affect only his attitude towards things abroad. Whatever touches the inner life of the soul of man here, and uplifts and enlarges it, is surely of influence on the Church here, and the Church here reaps an incalculable benefit. It has often been remarked that a Church which has not a wide enough outlook to take the world into her view cannot possibly have sufficient insight to deal with the souls of individuals, that a Church whose faith cannot grapple hopefully with world problems, certainly has not enough faith to deal with the problems of our great cities, that the Church which has no foreign policy is a Church whose home policy, if she has one, is necessarily weak. But all these sayings do but express different sides of the truth that men need a Christ who is larger than themselves, and a Hope which is fuller than their own individual salvation. A Gospel for England is no Gospel, a Christ for the white man is no Christ. Less than the whole is nothing. The moment we cease to reach out to the universal Hope we cease to reach out to the Hope at all. Thus it is manifest that to grapple with the task at home, to understand the work of the Church at home, certainly to take any active or intelligent part in its work, the wide and glorious Hope which comes to us from our missions is absolutely essential.

III. If a true understanding of the Hope before us reacts strongly upon our life at home, not less does an understanding of the use of means and external forms. Here at home the material aspect of things is constantly before our eyes. The organizations are so complete and so numerous, and we are so constantly asked to maintain them as external organizations, that, though the spiritual end is there, it is apt to be obscured, to be so overlaid as to escape observation. We are asked to give money to build churches, and to adorn them, to provide clubs, schools, and institutions of all kinds ; and these seem to be often ends in themselves. The one real end, the salvation of souls, the Revelation of Christ, is lost under the pile of its machinery, just as in some writings the argument is lost under the multiplicity of its exposition. Hardly do we get to the main purpose, by reason that we are constantly losing our way in the labyrinth in which it is set. Again and again we are so lost. The adornment of our buildings, the improvement of our organs and furniture, the multiplication of our organizations and their perfection assume an importance of their own. We work for them. Yet no one when he stops to think really believes that these things in themselves have any eternal value. Their sole value in the world of spirit lies in the Spirit which creates and is expressed by them and in their capacity to subserve that Spirit and so help others to find it.

Here we are lost often, but in missions not so often. Men do support missions for the most part with a spiritual end clear in view. It is the salvation of souls, the Revelation of Christ, which is constantly presented. We are often indeed asked to give all sorts of things, buildings and organizations and

ornaments, to Foreign Missions which do not
seem particularly well designed to attain that
Spiritual end ; we have sometimes set before
us views of missions which obscure it : but
still in the main it is true that people far
more easily escape out of the labyrinth in
their giving to missions than they do in
their giving to parochial objects.

But every time that we so escape, every
time that we get a clear view of the spiritual
end through the external form, we are drawn
upward and onward, we are rendered more
capable of the right use of means, we are
more likely to inquire into the real meaning
and purpose of gifts at home.   To find the
spiritual end in external acts once is to
get a new understanding of the meaning
of giving. It is people who so understand
that are the mainstay of all good works
at home, for there is no true giving without it.

The tendency to look on the outward things
which is so terribly dangerous at home is
strengthened by the very efficiency and com-

pleteness of the organization. Not only is
it constantly before our eyes; but it is
constantly before our eyes as on the whole
well designed and calculated to accomplish something. If we ask, To accomplish
what ? the answer is, A well organized
parish, a good club, a beautiful Service,
attractive and well attended. The arith-
metical sum recurs again and again. Given so
many men, so much money, the progress of
the Church is assured. And this in spite of the
fact that other voices are warning us that
the Church does not make progress as she
ought to do. Our common answer to that is an
appeal for more men, more money, better organization. I have already pointed out how
often and with what serious results we carry
this material attitude into our work abroad;
but abroad it is more easy to escape from it
than it is at home. There we are more often
forced back upon the truth. There the
organization is more obviously inadequate.
We escape by the joyful gate of despair.
We have happily still ringing in our ears the

scoffs and jibes of those who told us that "if God would make windows in heaven might this thing be." We have still some recollection that our hope that it would be, depended solely upon our conviction that God would make windows in heaven. We are forced back upon the Spirit. We see more clearly that the Spirit alone avails anything. We see that our only hope is to appeal to the Spirit, that the one thing needful is spiritual power. But this lesson, once learnt abroad, cannot but influence our action at home. When once we see that appeals for material are wholly inadequate, we begin to apply that apprehension to things at home, and we begin to understand that at home too, excellence of organization and abundance of supplies will of themselves not avail us. We do not give less, we give more, but what is of infinitely more importance, we give differently, and we use gifts differently, not differently externally, but internally. We cease to rely upon the material.

Because we cease to rely upon the material,

we see that motives are all important. It is the Spirit which matters. At home we often speak as if the motive from which gifts are made were the giver's private concern. We appeal for gifts, we welcome all gifts. We appeal to a man to give a site for a Church on the ground that it will increase the value of his property, as simply as we appeal for money to build the church on the ground that it will afford spiritual benefit to a large and growing population. The one motive and the other alike serve our turn. Then when the church is built we complain that the people do not use it or support it as well as they might. We do not see the connection between the foundation and the superstructure. The motive behind the gift is the real gift. It is far from being the giver's private concern, it concerns all to whom his gift comes. If there is a materialistic beginning, how can we expect anything but a materialistic end. Will the Devil allow us to use his weapons to fight against him ? Certainly he will, knowing that the more we appear to win against him the more he has us in his power, and the better we serve his ends. We are often caught in this snare at home, we are often caught in it abroad ; but abroad the importance of purity of motive more easily emerges, and the appeal for work abroad is more often made as an appeal to the higher motives. It is there that the appeal for spiritual men for spiritual work, and spiritual means for spiritual work, has been most strong. And if there is a tendency to-day to think more of the means and less of the Spirit, still it is in the mission field that the spiritual apprehension is most quick. There we cannot escape from the truth that the material cannot accomplish our purpose. And there above all we learn that we do not simply appeal to the Holy Spirit as an external force to use actions done without Him, but rather appeal to Him as indwelling those who act. Consequently we perceive that the motive is all important not only to him who acts, but to those towards whom he acts. And this once perceived, we proceed along the same line at home. What

we need in England is not large supplies
given from any motive, but a quickening of
Spirit. We can see that all efforts directed
to the procuring of material supplies which
do not begin with the stirring of the Spirit
are vain and dangerous. When our pastors
and teachers complain of the illiberality of
their congregations, the only hope of amendment lies not in more fervent appeals for
gifts, but in a renewal of the mind, a truer
presentation of the Gospel.

Further, at home the things which we are
asked to give are very largely things which
we can see. The warming, lighting, and de-
corating of churches, and such like works
occupy a large part of our attention. Here
we feel and see the effect of our gifts. It is a
very common complaint that our people will
give freely to things which they can see, but
things which they cannot see do not appeal to
them. Now all true giving is a form of
sacrifice, and much of this giving is rather
selfishness disguised. The things which we
give touch our own comfort and appeal to our

own senses. Nothing is really given till it is given away, but this giving is largely giving to ourselves. Yet we call it sacrifice; and sometimes there is, behind such giving, sacrifice of a higher order, but more often there is not. Thus the idea of Christian liberality as sacrifice is confused in our minds. We cease to know what is sacrifice, and what is not. We often deceive ourselves, thinking that we have given much when we have given nothing.

In giving to missions we escape from this snare also. We give outside our own immediate surroundings; we escape from local and personal considerations. We really give. Thus giving to missions is an invaluable lesson in the meaning of giving. This necessarily reacts upon all our giving at home. When once we have learnt the joy of sacrifice, the art of giving freely, without any expectation or desire of deriving any benefit for ourselves, simply for the love of Christ, we become more capable of giving truly at home. We cease to demand a return for our gifts in some tangible, visible result.

Freed from this craving for tangible results, the lust of the eye, we can more readily distinguish important from unimportant, essential from trivial, objects. Very often the things which are most readily, almost eagerly, supplied, are those things which really affect the progress of the Gospel least. We often complain of the lamentable waste which goes on. Large amounts of useful material are spent in supplying things which afford pleasure but for a short time and then become a burden, or an offence. It is true that it is possible to express a real devotion in adorning the walls of a building with the works of a third-rate artist. It is a dangerous thing to call it " waste." It may be anything but waste. Nevertheless, though it may not be waste, yet it often is waste ; and in any case, when things of serious, if not vital, importance are left undone whilst these are done, it argues a lamentable lack of judgment. If it may be true to say, " These ought ye to have done," it is certainly true to say, " The other ye ought not to have left undone." Not to be able to distinguish great from small is not a light failing. Clergy and laity alike, we all fail ; and we fail largely because we look on the outward things and are the slaves of the lust of the eye. We dare not face the matter and ask what it really is.

But when we have once learnt to give, when we have once known giving as the necessary expression in act of an impelling Spirit of Redeeming Love which demands a form, then we begin to learn both to pay slight heed to the seen, and to measure all forms of expression by their utility, or capacity, or fitness as instruments of that Spirit of Redeeming Love. Then we begin to distinguish. The one question with us is no longer what benefit, or what pleasure, we shall derive from the sight of our gift in use, but what gift is most becoming to the Spirit which urges us to sacrifice. Instantly the really important things appear clearly in their importance.

Our eyes are enlightened; we learn to know
great from small.

If these things are so, it is not surprising
that the cultivation and exercise of the
Missionary Spirit should be a most powerful
aid to progress at home. That it is so is
constantly asserted and has been often proved
by experience. Canon Body was wont to
say of his country parish in Yorkshire that
" he considered that all the blessing which
manifestly rested upon that parish during the
years that he was there, was directly traceable
to the devotional spirit in which the work of
Foreign Missions was done." Dr. Eugene
Stock in his *History of the Church Missionary Society* [1] shows the close connection between the growth of missionary zeal and the
uplifting of the Church at home. " It was
the parishes in which zeal and interest in the
evangelisation of the world were manifested
that were at the front in all church work at
home." Canon Brooke, of St. John the
Divine, Kennington, a few days before his

[1] I. 275.

death, told us what was the effect produced in that parish by the surrender of one of their clergy with his stipend to the service of God in Canada. "Our collections in church, our subscriptions to our home charities have been greater during the last three months. It pays also in spiritual power and interest: there has been a general leavening up of the whole congregation." A cloud of witnesses could be cited. The saying is commonplace amongst the supporters of Foreign Missions. Nevertheless, it has not yet been generally accepted either by the parochial clergy, or by churchwardens, or by the members of our congregations. They still constantly look simply at the outward things and imagine that help given to Foreign Missions, or money given "out of the parish" is so much loss. They cannot grasp the fundamental necessity of seeing far, in order to understand things at home. They are like some teachers in elementary schools who, beginning the study of geography with the school and its yard, never get beyond the yard. As in geography " it

is of the essence of the modern standpoint
that no area can be understood without
reference to the world at large," [1] so it is of
the essence of Christian knowledge that no
detail of the sphere of the Spirit's work can be
understood without reference to the whole.
The nature and work and character of the
Spirit cannot be apprehended or accepted as
long as the eyes of the mind are fixed on
merely local conditions.

It cannot have escaped observation that
in writing of missionary principles, I have
been writing of principles which have a wider
application than to Foreign Missions. The
principles could be applied to any work anywhere. All that I insist upon here is that
they are world-wide. And it is from the
world-wide outlook that we can alone reach
them, grasp them, and learn to apply them
anywhere. The apprehension of them has
come to us from missionary work all over the
world. It is a reaction, and that reaction is
inevitable, certain, and of incalculable value

[1] *Modern Geography*, p. 17.

to us at home. If only we could persuade ourselves of this truth not only would the cause of missions everywhere be advanced, but we should all have made a great step forward.